W9-BFY-701

Big Book of Bible Crafts

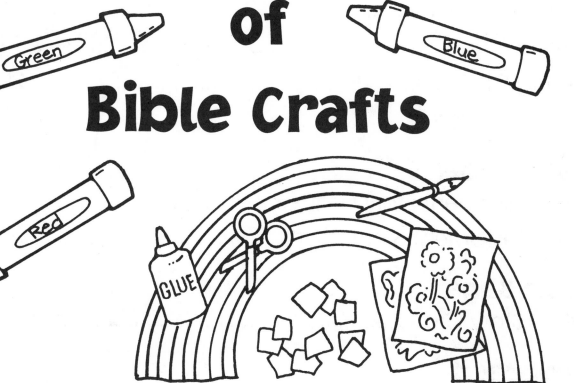

Cover Illustration by Janet Skiles
Cover Production by Nehmen-Kodner

This book is a compilation of previously published materials.

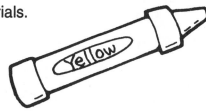

All rights reserved—Printed in the U.S.A.
Copyright © 1998 Shining Star Publications
A Division of Frank Schaffer Publications, Inc.
23740 Hawthorne Blvd., Torrance, CA 90505

Notice! Pages may be reproduced for home or classroom use only, not for commercial resale. No part of this publication may be reproduced for storage in a retrieval system, or transmitted in any form or by any means—electronic, mechanical, recording, etc.—without the prior written permission of the publisher. Reproduction of these materials for an entire school or school system is strictly prohibited.

Unless otherwise indicated, the New International Version of the Bible was used in preparing the activities in this book. Scripture taken from the HOLY BIBLE, NEW INTERNATIONAL VERSION. Copyright © 1973, 1978, 1984 International Bible Society. Used by permission of Zondervan Bible Publishers.

Table of Contents

Introduction 3

Paper Plates
Autumn Crafts 4–11

Winter Crafts..12–19

Spring Crafts 20–29

Summer Crafts..30–40

Tissue Paper
Old Testament Story Crafts 41–54

New Testament Story Crafts 55–79

Paper Bags
Bible Story Crafts 80–117

Cardboard
Old Testament Story Crafts 118–129

New Testament Story Crafts 130–160

© Shining Star Publications

SS20001

Introduction

Big Book of Bible Crafts is filled with a wonderful variety of simple craft projects children can do to learn all about the Bible and God's love for us! Children will have all kinds of fun making puppets, masks, plaques, posters, snowmen, angels, baskets, rainbows, wreaths, ornaments, and so much more!

Each craft is based on a Bible story or Christian value and many contain a Bible verse. Discuss these concepts and read the stories from the Bible with the children. Help the children understand their importance in their lives.

Paper plates, paper bags, tissue paper, and cardboard are the main materials needed for the crafts, in addition to other easily-available materials. Step-by-step directions for the children and any necessary patterns are included. While the majority of the projects can be completed without adult supervision, several do require an adult's help.

You will love watching the children have fun creating many wonderful works of art as they come to better understand the Bible and God's all-powerful love for us.

© Shining Star Publications

3

Painted Pumpkin

Materials:

two 8" paper plates, orange paint, paintbrushes, green paint or crayons, scissors, glue, copy of the stem and phrase below

Directions:

1. Paint the bottoms of both plates orange and allow to dry.

2. Color or paint the stem pattern green. Fold on the dotted lines and glue together.

3. Apply glue to the tab on the stem. Glue it to the inside rim of one of the plates. Glue the front rims of the plates together.

4. Color and cut out the phrase.

5. Paste it to one side of the pumpkin.

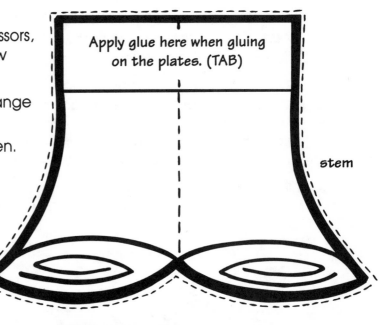

Apply glue here when gluing on the plates. (TAB)

stem

GREAT IS THE LORD

© Shining Star Publications

4

SS20001

Give thanks to the Lord, call on his name; make known among the nations what he has done.
(1 Chronicles 16:8)

Turkey Time

Materials:
one 8" paper plate, crayons or felt-tip markers, scissors, glue, construction paper of various colors, patterns below and on page 6

Directions:

2. and 3.

1. Color the bottom of the paper plate brown.

2. Color and cut out the turkey head pattern on page 6. Fold on the dotted line. Glue it to the center of the back of the paper plate.

3. Color the feet patterns yellow, cut them out, and glue them to the bottom of the turkey.

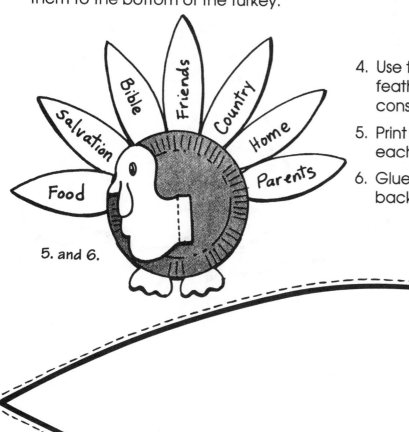

4. Use the feather pattern to trace 6–7 feathers on various colors of construction paper. Cut them out.

5. Print something you are thankful for on each feather.

6. Glue the feathers around the rim on the back of the turkey.

5. and 6.

feather

© Shining Star Publications

SS20001

Patterns

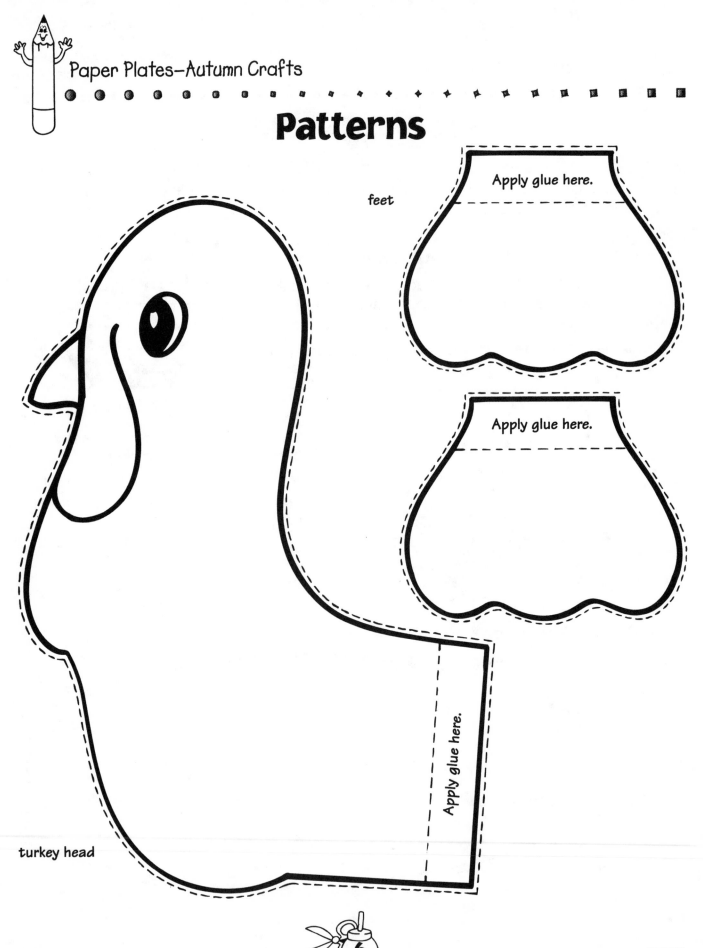

feet

Apply glue here.

Apply glue here.

Apply glue here.

turkey head

© Shining Star Publications

6

SS20001

"Ask and it will be given to you; seek and you will find; knock and the door will be opened to you."
(Matthew 7:7)

God Answers Prayers

Materials:
two 8" paper plates, felt-tip marker, scissors, glue, pattern below

Directions:

1. Cut out and trace the pattern on one of the paper plates.

2. Reverse the pattern and trace it on the other plate.

3. Outline the pattern you traced with a felt-tip marker and cut, leaving the outline.

4. Glue the backs together, applying glue only behind the lady and the chair.

5. Print "God Answers Prayers" on the bottom of the rocker. The rocker should stand up by itself and rock.

4.

GOD ANSWERS PRAYERS

Place on edge of plate.

© Shining Star Publications

SS20001

Wise Old Owl

Materials:

two 8" paper plates, crayons or felt-tip markers, scissors, glue, copies of the patterns below and on pages 9–11

Directions:

1. Color the bottoms of both paper plates brown.

2. Glue them together as shown, overlapping about 1".

3. Color and cut out all of the patterns.

4. Glue the patterns onto each paper plate as directed:

   a. Glue the forehead to the top of the plate.

   b. Glue the beak as shown.

   c. Add the eyes.

   d. Glue the wings on the bottom plate. Glue the Bible inside the wings to look as if the owl is holding it.

   e. Add the tail to the bottom and glue the feet to make the owl look like it is sitting on a branch.

This project is great for a back-to-school project!

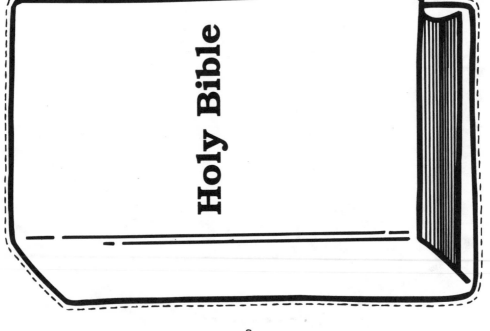

Holy Bible

© Shining Star Publications

SS20001

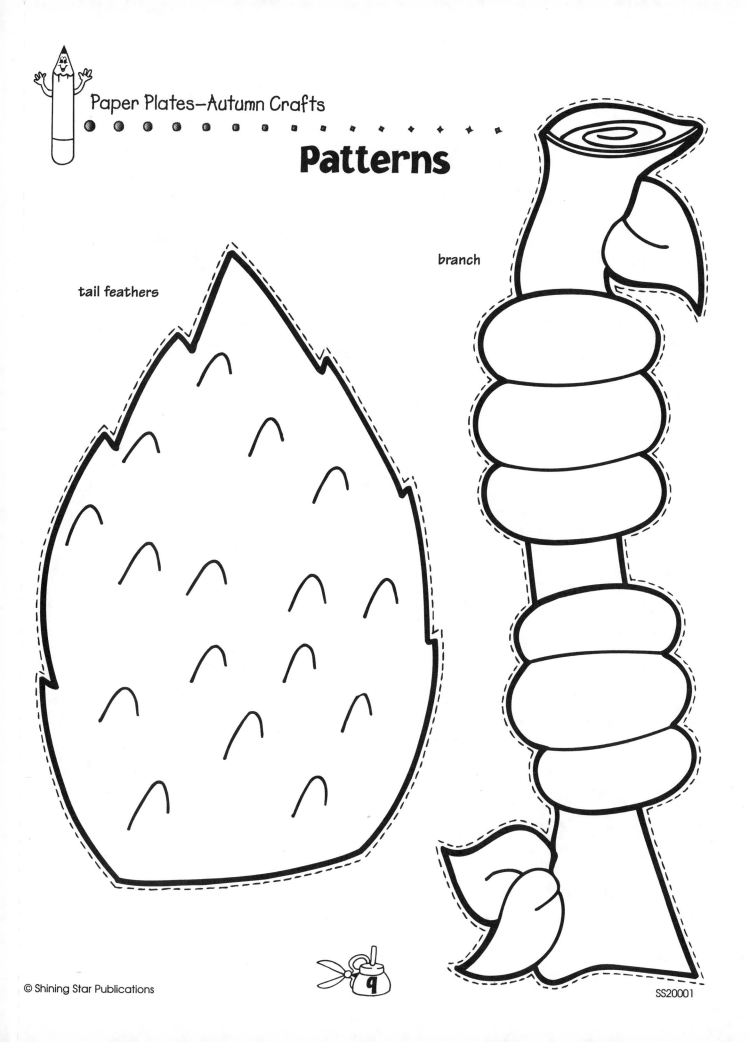

Paper Plates—Autumn Crafts

Patterns

tail feathers

branch

© Shining Star Publications

9

SS20001

Patterns

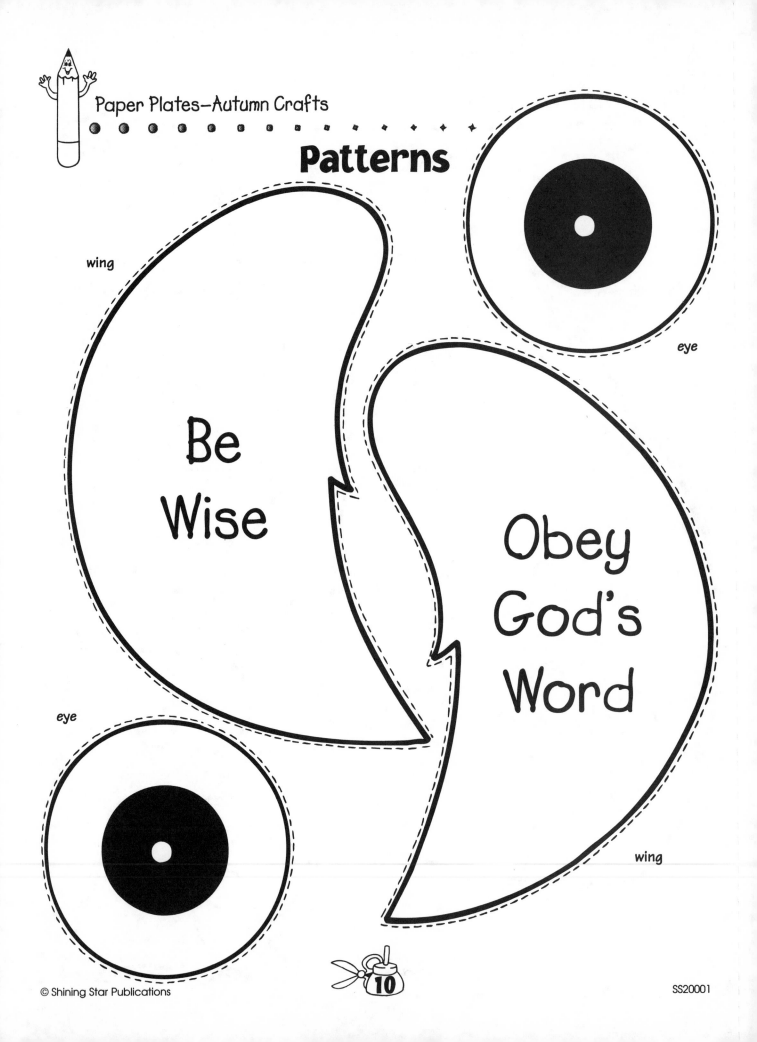

wing

eye

Be Wise

eye

Obey God's Word

wing

© Shining Star Publications

10

SS20001

Patterns

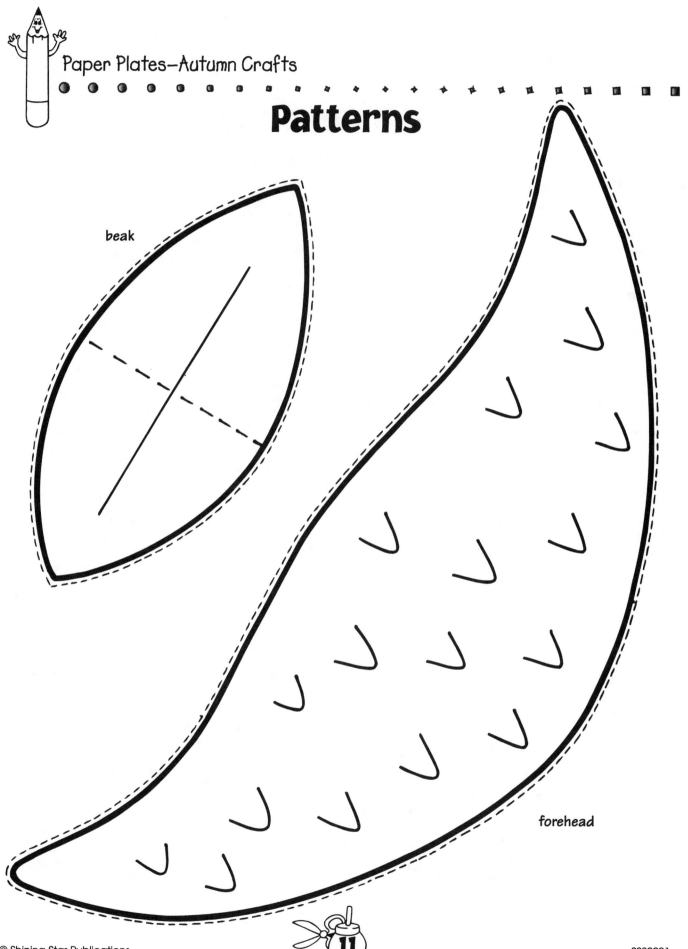

beak

forehead

© Shining Star Publications

11

SS20001

"Glory to God in the highest, and on earth peace to men on whom his favor rests." (Luke 2:14)

Christmas Bells

Materials:

one 8" paper plate, glue, scissors, aluminum foil, ribbon or yarn, patterns below

Directions:

1. Cut the paper plate in half.

2. Cut aluminum foil pieces the size of both paper plate halves and glue them to the back side of each plate. Let dry until aluminum foil adheres to paper plate halves.

3. Roll one half into a cone shape, overlapping and gluing where needed.

4. Repeat the above directions for the other half of the paper plate.

5. Color the patterns and cut them out. Glue one pattern onto each bell.

6. Make a hole at the tip of each bell. Thread ribbon or yarn through the hole of each bell. Tie ribbon or yarn into a bow to hang the bells.

1.

2.

3.

4.

6.

5.

Ring the bells, Christ was born in Bethlehem!

5.

© Shining Star Publications

12

SS20001

An angel of the Lord appeared to them, and the glory of the Lord shone around them . . . (Luke 2:9)

Angel of Love

Materials:

one 8" paper plate, crayons, scissors, glue, patterns below

Directions:

1. Cut the paper plate in half. Roll one of the halves into a cone shape. Glue to hold.

2. Cut the other plate half in half again to form two quarter sections. Overlap slightly and glue to form sleeves.

3. Color and cut out the patterns. Fold on the dotted lines.

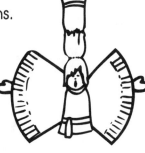

4. Insert the sleeves inside the folded area of the angel. Glue to hold. Glue hands to sleeves.

5. Apply glue on the inside of the waist and skirt area of the angel. Set on top of the cone and press firmly to glue to the cone.

6. Bend arms forward.

Apply glue behind these areas when fastening to sleeves.

Apply glue behind this area when fastening to the cone.

hands

© Shining Star Publications

13

SS20001

Paper Plates—Winter Crafts

Christmas Wreath

Materials:
two 8" paper plates, green construction paper, crayons, scissors, glue, patterns below and on page 15

Directions:

1. Cut out the center of one of the paper plates, leaving a 1 ½" rim around the edge.

2. Cut out the holly leaf pattern. Trace around it 20 times onto green construction paper. Cut out the leaves.

3. Glue the leaves in an attractive arrangement around the rim of the plate, overlapping leaves slightly to completely cover the rim.

4. Cut out the bow pattern. Color it red. Paste it on the wreath as shown above. (Or, if desired, cut a bow out of red construction paper.)

5. Color the manger pattern and cut it out.

6. Glue it in the center on the front of the second plate.

7. Glue the two plates together with the front rims facing each other.

manger

© Shining Star Publications

14

SS20001

Patterns

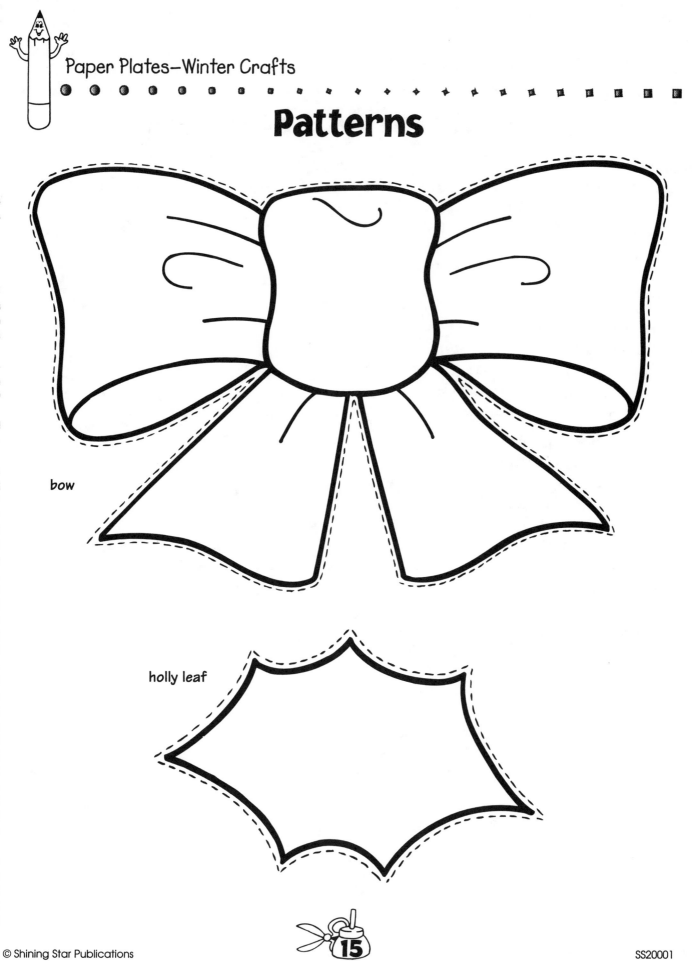

bow

holly leaf

© Shining Star Publications

SS20001

Snowflake Fun

Materials:
two 8" white paper plates, hole punch, sharp scissors, dark blue crayon, silver glitter, glue, white thread, large sheet of paper, patterns

Directions:

1. Cut out the two snowflake patterns. Trace pattern 1 onto the center of a paper plate and cut it out.

   Cut out here.

2. Trace around pattern 2 onto the center of the other paper plate and cut it out.

3. Using a paper punch, make holes where indicated on the small loose snowflake.

4. Punch a hole above the cutout pattern 1 on the paper plate. Tie a short length of thread between pattern 2 and the plate, allowing pattern 2 to swing freely.

5. Using a dark blue crayon, print neatly around the border of the plate:
   . . . wash me, and I will be whiter than snow.

6. Lay the project on the large sheet of paper. Apply glue at various places on the snowflake and sprinkle glitter over the glue. Gently shake off excess glitter onto the paper.

7. Attach another length of thread at the top for a hanger.

pattern 2

pattern 1

WASH ME AND I WILL BE WHITER THAN SNOW

16

© Shining Star Publications

"Be still, and know that I am God . . ."
(Psalm 46:10)

A Merry Mouse

Materials:

two 8" paper plates, crayons or felt-tip markers, scissors, glue, yarn or thin rope, patterns below

Directions:

1. Cut one of the paper plates in half.

2. Glue the front sides of the plate halves together. Cut a slit through both thicknesses of the paper plates, about one-third of the way in, as indicated.

3. Draw and color two eyes and a nose. (If desired, add whiskers made from broom straws and glue them into place.)

4. Trace around the ear pattern twice on the other plate and cut them out. Insert the ears into the slits on the body of the mouse.

5. Glue on a short length of yarn or rope for a tail.

6. Cut out the the wording and glue it to one side of the mouse. Print "Be quiet as a mouse" on the other side. The mouse should be able to sit up.

5.

4.

2.

ear

Reverse here
for other ear.

Fold.

Study To
Be Quiet

Place against
side of plate.

17

© Shining Star Publications

SS20001

Valentine Holder

Materials:
two 8" paper plates; crayons; scissors; glue; hole punch;
red, pink, or white yarn; patterns below and on page 19

Directions:
1. Cut out the pocket pattern on page 19 and trace around it on one of the paper plates. Cut it out.

2. Glue the pocket to the other paper plate with the fronts of the plates together. Apply glue to the rims of the plates.

3. Color the valentine decoration patterns. Cut them out and glue them in an attractive arrangement on the front of the holder.

4. Use the hole punch to make holes evenly around the edge of the holder. Starting on the top, lace yarn through each hole. When you have gone completely around the holder, tie the yarn at the top in a pretty bow. If you plan to hang the holders, allow extra yarn for a loop.

1.

2.

. . . direct your hearts into God's love . . .
(2 Thessalonians 3:5)

Love never fails.

A friend loves at all times.

© Shining Star Publications

SS20001

Patterns

Jesus loves me!

© Shining Star Publi

SS20001

" . . . Let them rise up to help you!
Let them give you shelter!"
(Deuteronomy 32:38)

A Useful Umbrella

Materials:

one large paper plate, glue, scissors, crayons, light blue construction paper, white thread, one drinking straw, tape, raindrop pattern below

Directions:

1. Color the bottom of the paper plate any color desired.

2. Cut a slit in the paper plate halfway to the center.

3. Roll the paper plate to form a cone shape. Glue to hold. Write "God Protects" on the top of the plate.

4. Tape the drinking straw to the center of the cone shape (umbrella) to form the handle.

5. Cut out the raindrop pattern. Trace around it onto the light blue construction paper 5–7 times and cut them out. On each drop, list one thing that God gives us to show us that He cares about us.

6. Hang the drops around the edge of the umbrella using white thread. Stagger the lengths of the thread to make the drops look more realistic.

These umbrellas may be used as mobiles.

raindrop

© Shining Star Publications

SS20001

Easter Lily

Materials:
one 8" paper plate, scissors, glue, crayons, paper, patterns below and on pages 22–23

Directions:

1. Cut a paper plate in half.

2. Cut out the lily pattern (page 23) and trace around it onto half of a paper plate. Cut it out.

3. Roll the lily pattern into a cone shape to form a flower. Glue to hold in place.

4. Color the flower center pattern (below). Cut it out on the bold lines. Fold it into quarters and fluff slightly. Glue it in the center of the lily.

5. Make three copies of the leaf pattern (page 23). Color them green and cut them out.

6. Color purple the border around the "Christ Arose!" poster (page 22).

7. Glue the leaves on the lower right corner of the poster, applying glue only at the base of the leaves.

Christ Arose!

8. Glue the lily on top of the leaves as shown.

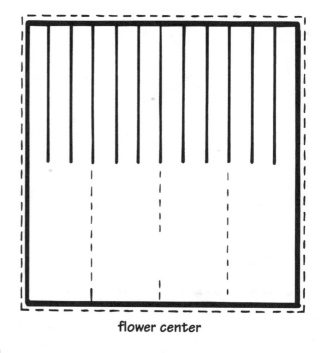

flower center

Christ Arose!

Apply glue here.

© Shining Star Publications

22

SS20001

"I have set my rainbow in the clouds, and it will be the sign of the covenant between me and the earth." (Genesis 9:13)

A Special Rainbow

Materials:

one 8" paper plate, glue, scissors, crayons, string, hole punch, cotton balls, patterns below

Directions:

1. Cut about a 2"–2½" wide strip off the outer rim of the paper plate. Then cut off about one-third of the rim.

2. Color it to resemble a rainbow.

3. Cut out the clouds below and glue one on each end of the rainbow. Behind each cloud, glue on some fluffed up cotton.

4. Make a hole at the top of the rainbow and attach a short string to form a hanger.

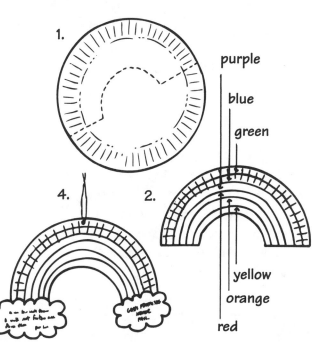

"... I will be with you; I will never leave you nor forsake you." (Joshua 1:5)

God's Promises Never Fail!

© Shining Star Publications

27

SS20001

© Shin

. . . "Your servant has been keeping his father's sheep. When a lion or a bear came and carried off a sheep . . . I went after it . . ." (1 Samuel 17:34–35)

Lion and Lamb Fun

Materials:
two 8" paper plates, yellow yarn, cotton balls, glue, scissors, crayons

Directions:

LION

1. Draw a face on a paper plate as shown. Draw a triangle in the middle of the plate. Add eyes and a mouth. Draw ears as indicated. Add eyelashes, whiskers, and other details.

2. Cut short lengths of yellow yarn (about 2" lengths) and glue them around the rim of the plate for a mane.

1.

2.

LAMB

3. Draw a lamb's face on another paper plate as shown, making a round nose and eyes and long, fluffy ears.

4. Fluff up cotton balls and glue them on the forehead of the lamb.

5. A Bible verse can be printed on the back sides of the lion and the lamb. Pick a verse that is in accordance with the story being told or Scripture being studied.

© Shining Star Publications

SS20001

Paper Plates—Spring Crafts

Mother's Day Basket

Materials:

two 8" paper plates; glue; crayons; scissors; silk, paper, or plastic flowers; pencil; ribbon; pattern below

Directions:

1. Cut one paper plate in half. (Discard one of the halves or share it with someone else.)

2. With a pencil, divide the other paper plate in half. Then draw a one-inch border around one half as shown. Cut out the inside of this section.

Cut out this area.

3. Glue the half plate to the bottom of the second plate to form a basket shape. Color the rims.

4. Color and cut out the pattern. Paste it on the bottom of the basket.

5. If desired, fill the basket with flowers. Use ribbon to tie a pretty bow on the handle.

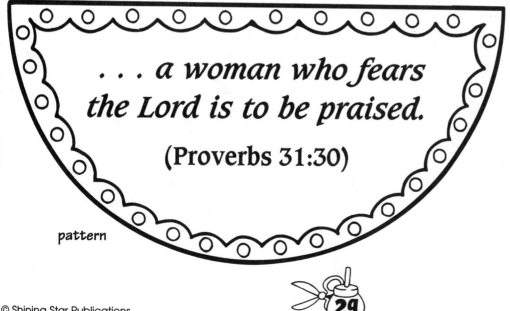

. . . *a woman who fears the Lord is to be praised.*

(Proverbs 31:30)

pattern

29

© Shining Star Publications

SS20001

Both of them were upright in the sight of God, observing all the Lord's commandments . . .
(Luke 1:6)

A Lucky Ladybug

Materials:
three 8" paper plates, black and red paint, paintbrushes, scissors, glue, patterns below

Directions:

1. Paint the bottoms of two of the paper plates black.

2. Cut out the ladybug's head. Apply glue on the tab and attach it to the inner rim of one of the plates.

3. Paste the other painted plate behind the first with the fronts of the plates together.

4. Cut out wings from the third plate as shown. Paint them red. Apply glue under the wings, near the head area only, and glue them to the top of the ladybug, allowing the wings to stick up a little.

5. Cut out and glue the word dots below onto the body of the ladybug.

head

TAB

Walk

with

the

Lord

© Shining Star Publications

SS20001

". . . let your light shine before men, that they may see your deeds and praise your Father in heaven." (Matthew 5:16)

A Super Summer Sun

Materials:

two 8" paper plates, crayons or felt-tip markers, scissors, glue, yellow construction paper, patterns below

Directions:

1. Color the bottoms of the paper plates yellow.

2. Cut out the sunbeam pattern and trace it 14 or more times onto yellow construction paper.

3. Cut out the sunbeams and glue them evenly around the front rim of one of the plates. Glue the fronts of the two plates together.

4. Color and cut out the saying below. Glue it to the center of the sun on one side.

sunbeam

Other Idea:

On each sunbeam, list a way we can let our lives shine for Jesus.

4.

LET YOUR LIFE SHINE FOR JESUS

© Shining Star Publications

31

SS20001

Be kind and compassionate to one another, forgiving each other . . .
(Ephesians 4:32)

A Fantastic Fan

Materials:
one 8" paper plate, one craft stick, glue, scissors, crayons, sayings below

Directions:
1. Cut the paper plate exactly in half.
2. Glue the bottoms together with the craft stick in the middle.
3. Color as desired.
4. Color and cut out the sayings below. Glue one on each side of the fan.

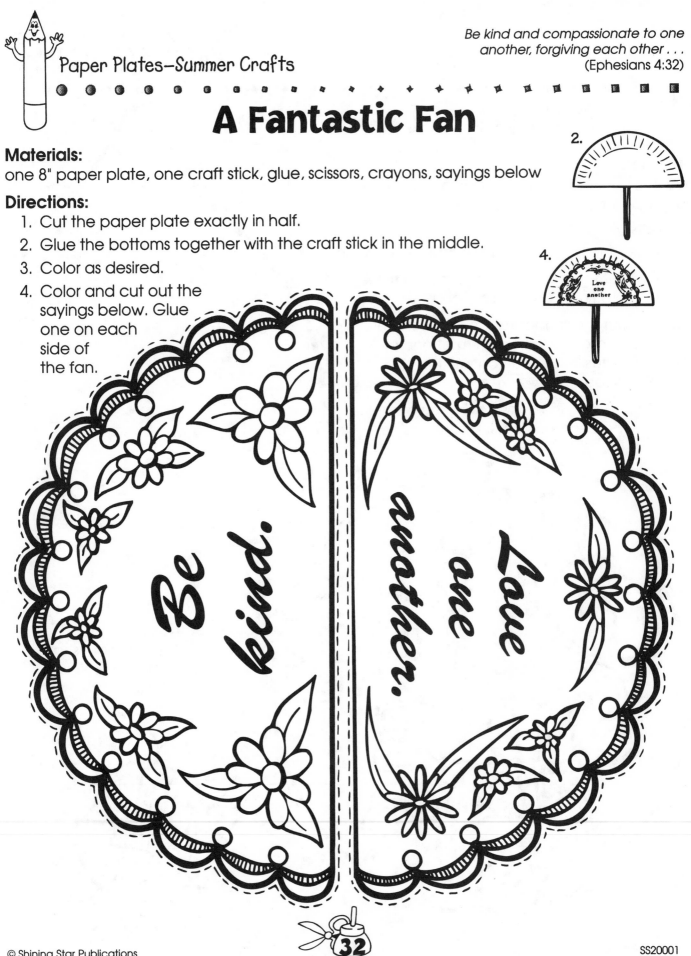

Be kind.

Love one another.

© Shining Star Publications

SS20001

Taste and see that the Lord is good;
blessed is the man who takes
refuge in him. (Psalm 34:8)

Watermelon Slice

Materials:

one 8" paper plate; crayons, paints and paintbrushes, or felt-tip markers; dried watermelon seeds; glue

Directions:

1. Color the front of a paper plate to resemble a watermelon slice, as indicated.

2. Fold the plate in half so it will stand.

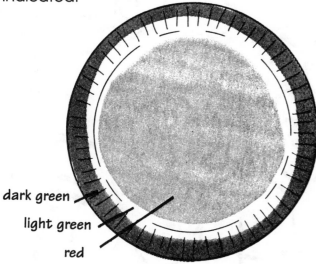

dark green
light green
red

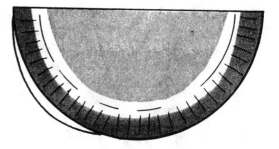

3. Using a black pen, print the following Bible verse and reference on the watermelon slice (or one similar to it): *Taste and see that the Lord is good . . .* (Psalm 34:8)

4. Glue on a few seeds for a realistic look.

© Shining Star Publications

33

SS20001

I will be glad and rejoice in you; I will sing praise to your name, O Most High.
(Psalm 9:2)

An Important Balloon

Materials:

two 8" paper plates, crayons or felt-tip markers, glue, string (about a 15" length), pattern below

Directions:

1. Color the bottoms of both paper plates.

2. Glue the front rims together, inserting a string in one end to resemble a string tied to a balloon.

3. Color the saying below. Cut it out and paste it on the center of one side of the balloon.

God's LOVE is higher than the heavens

34

© Shining Star Publications

SS20001

Patterns

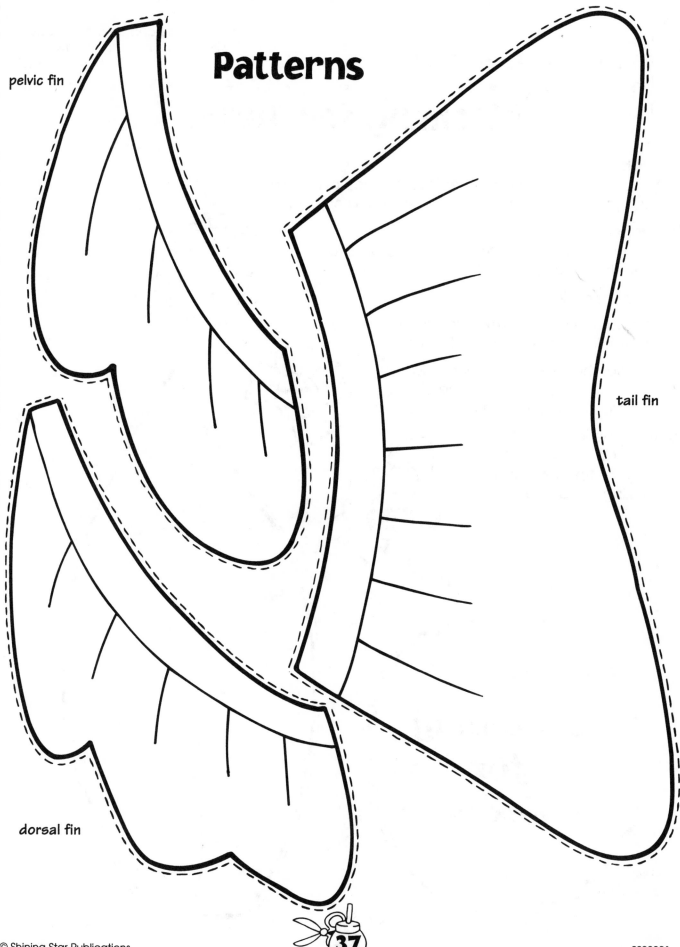

pelvic fin

tail fin

dorsal fin

37

© Shining Star Publications

SS20001

Blooming for Jesus

Materials:

one 8" paper plate, scissors, green construction paper, glue, crayons or felt-tip markers, patterns below and on page 39

Directions:

1. Cut out the flower pattern and trace around it onto the paper plate.

2. Color as desired.

3. Cut out the flower center and color it yellow. Paste it in the center of the flower.

4. Cut out the leaf pattern and trace around it three times onto the green construction paper. Cut out the leaves.

5. Glue the leaves behind the flower in a triangular shape, with the tips of the leaves sticking out a little.

flower center

Blooming for Jesus

leaf

38

© Shining Star Publications

SS20001

Pattern

flower

39

© Shining Star Publications

SS20001

Our Lord, a Shield

Materials:

one 8" paper plate, crayons or felt-tip markers, scissors, glue, lightweight cardboard, pattern below, aluminum foil (optional)

Directions:

1. Color the bottom of the paper plate as desired. Or, glue aluminum foil to the bottom of the plate.

2. Cut out the shield pattern and paste it in the center of the paper plate.

3. From lightweight cardboard, cut a 1½" x 7" strip. Glue it to the front side of the plate, which is the back side of the shield. Fold the cardboard as shown to form a handle.

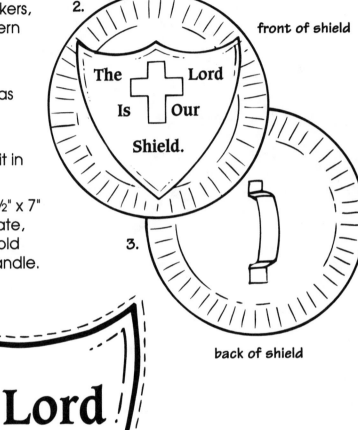

front of shield

back of shield

The Lord
Is ✝ Our
Shield.

shield

© Shining Star Publications

40

SS20001

. . . God created the heavens and the earth.
(Genesis 1:1)

Our Beautiful World Plaque

Materials:
blue and green tissue paper, paper plate, white glue and water in equal parts, sponge brush, markers

Directions:
1. Tear tissue into 1" to 2" pieces.

2. Brush the glue and water mixture over the center of the plate.

3. Glue the torn tissue down in the center of the plate. Overlap the tissue pieces as you place them over the glue.

4. Brush the glue mixture over the tissue pieces.

5. Use markers to write "God Made Our Beautiful World" around the rim.

Make a mobile!

Other Ideas:
1. Use plain water on top of the torn tissue paper. Pull the tissue pieces off when dry.

2. Follow the directions above and cover the centers of both sides of the plate and hang it for a mobile.

3. Cut paper or use markers to outline specific continents.

© Shining Star Publications

41

SS20001

Tissue Paper–Old Testament

Lights in the Sky Mobile

Materials:
yellow, orange, and white tissue paper; construction paper; scissors; markers or crayons; pencil; dowel stick; yarn or string; glue; hole punch; patterns on page 43

Directions:
1. Cut out the patterns.

2. Trace around the patterns on construction paper and cut them out.

3. Write "God's Lights" around the sun, "in the" around the star, and "Sky" around the moon.

4. Use orange tissue paper for the sun, white tissue paper for the moon, and yellow tissue paper for the star. Lightly trace the inside of each shape on the tissue. Cut the tissue paper shapes out about ½" larger than the outlines.

5. Turn each construction paper shape over and cover the hole in the middle of each shape by gluing the piece of tissue paper over it.

6. Punch a hole in each shape and tie it to the dowel stick with yarn or string.

7. Tie a string to the center of the dowel and hang your mobile as a reminder of the lights God has placed in the sky for you to see.

Other Ideas:
1. Draw your own patterns for the sun, moon, and star.

2. Make more stars and add them to the mobile. Leave the center in one star and write the words "God's Lights in the Sky" on it.

3. Outline the sun, moon, and star with glitter.

4. Instead of a mobile, do individual patterns for sun catchers.

© Shining Star Publications

SS20001

Patterns

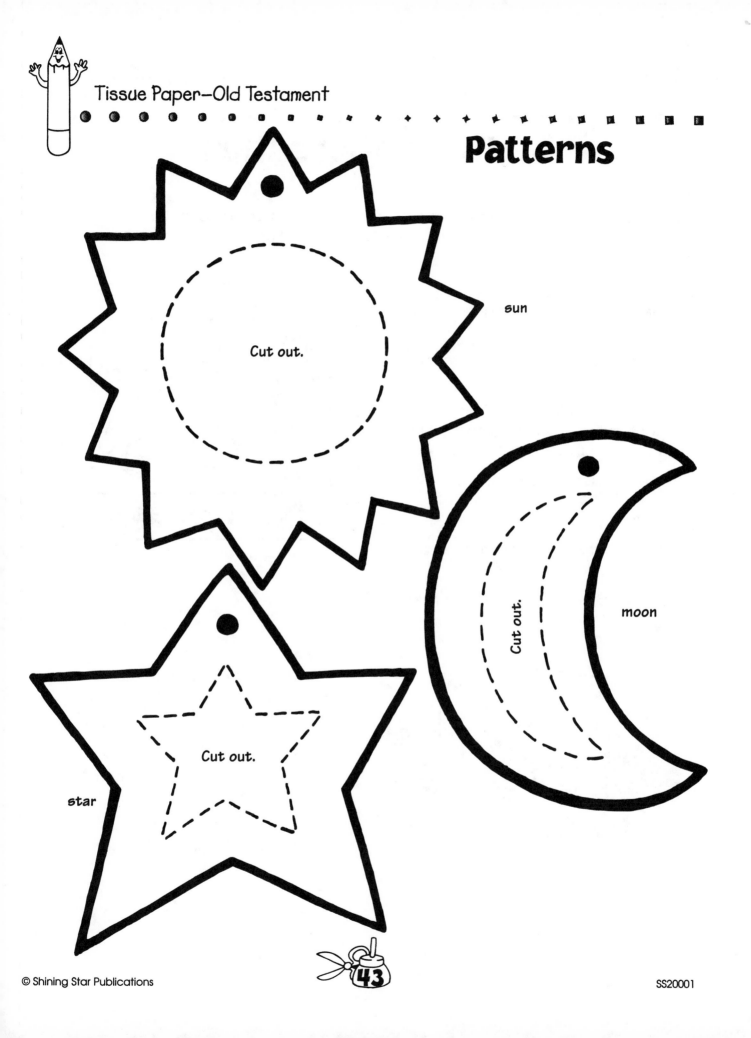

sun

Cut out.

moon

Cut out.

Cut out.

star

© Shining Star Publications

43

SS20001

. . . "Let the land produce vegetation: seed-bearing plants and trees . . ." (Genesis 1:11)

God's Plant Creation

Materials:
white or light-colored tissue paper, leaves, waxed paper, white glue and water in equal parts, sponge brush, iron, construction paper, two sheets of paper, scissors, markers

Directions:

God's Plant Creation

1. Cut a sheet of waxed paper and tissue paper to the same desired size.

2. Dip leaves into the glue and water mixture. Then place them on waxed paper.

3. Brush a layer of the glue and water mixture over the picture, cover it with the piece of tissue paper, and let dry.

4. Place the picture between the two sheets of paper, and iron it with a cool iron.

5. Cut a construction paper frame and glue it around the picture.

6. Write "God's Plant Creation" on the frame.

I hope you feel better!

Other Ideas:

1. Use pressed tissue to make get-well cards to give to shut-ins.

2. Add yarn, glitter, and other decorative materials.

3. Press flowers and add them to the picture.

4. Write a Bible verse about Creation on the picture frame.

© Shining Star Publications

SS20001

. . . "Let the land produce living creatures . . ." (Genesis 1:24)

Four-Footed Friends

Materials:
tissue paper in white and assorted colors, string, pipe cleaners, glue, scissors

Directions:
1. Choose an animal to make.

2. Crush white tissue paper into a ball. Tie off the head with a piece of string.

string

3. Wrap pipe cleaners around the animal's body for legs.

pipe cleaner

4. Fill out the legs with 1" x 12" strips of white tissue paper.

5. Glue 1" x 12" strips of colored tissue paper over the animal, adding features as desired.

6. Thank God for the many wonderful animals He has made.

Try making a turtle!

Other Ideas:
1. Omit pipe cleaners; roll up and cover white paper for legs.

2. Use a rubber band instead of string to tie off the animal's head.

3. Make a diorama of different animals, or make duplicate animals to go on an ark.

4. Use this technique to make animals that illustrate other Bible stories.

© Shining Star Publications

SS20001

"I have set my rainbow in the clouds . . ." (Genesis 9:13)

Noah's Mosaic Rainbow

Materials:
tissue paper in brown and assorted colors, scissors, white glue and water in equal parts, white paper, sponge brush, pencil, patterns on page 47

Directions:
1. Cut out the ark and land patterns. Trace around and cut out these patterns from brown tissue paper.

2. Cut squares from different colors of tissue paper. (Use ½" x ½" squares for an 8½" x 11" sheet of paper, and 1" x 1" squares for a larger sheet of paper.)

3. Brush the glue and water mixture on the paper.

4. Place the land and ark near the bottom of the picture.

5. Place the tissue squares above the ark to make a rainbow.

6. Brush over the tissue with another layer of glue and water. Then let it dry.

7. Write "God Keeps His Promises!" on the picture.

Other Ideas:
1. Cut out your own pattern for the ark and land.

2. Glue the tissue paper on a paper plate.

3. Draw an outline of the ark and land on the paper and fill them in with brown tissue paper squares.

4. Add pieces of blue tissue paper to make the sky behind the ark and rainbow.

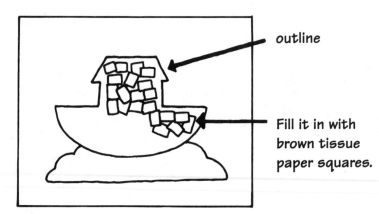

outline

Fill it in with brown tissue paper squares.

© Shining Star Publications

SS20001

Patterns

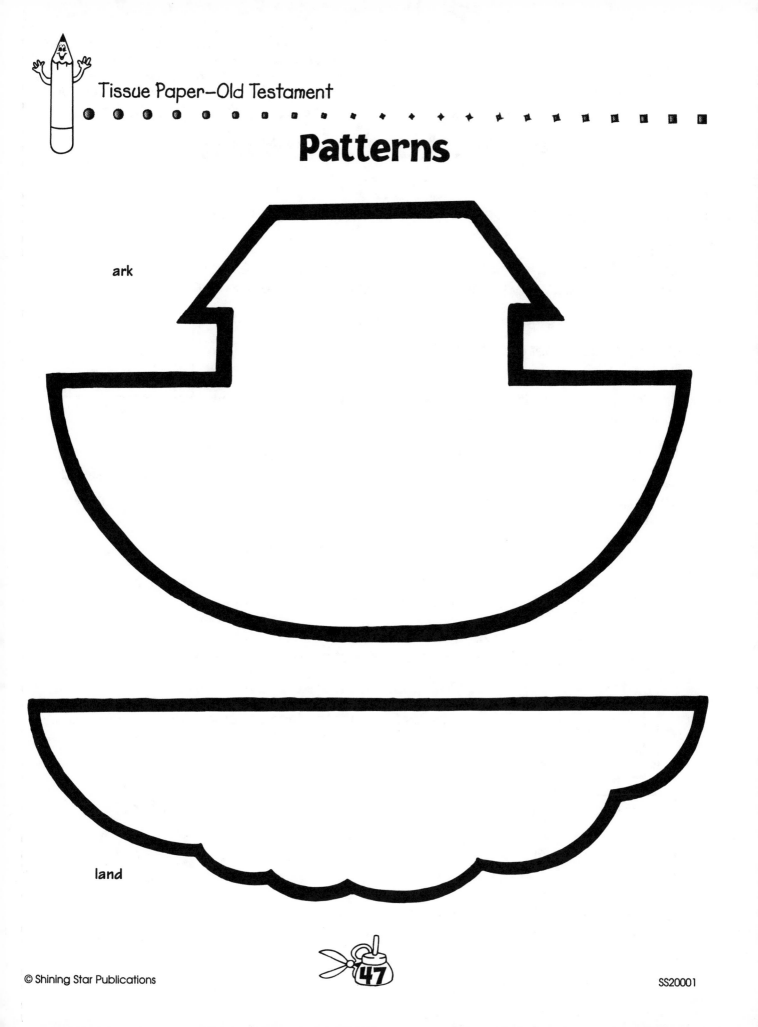

ark

land

© Shining Star Publications

SS20001

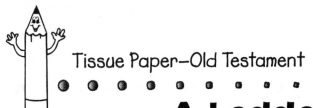

Tissue Paper–Old Testament

He (Jacob) had a dream in which he saw a stairway resting on the earth, with its top reaching to heaven, and the angels of God were ascending and descending on it. (Genesis 28:12)

A Ladder to Heaven

Materials:
tissue paper in white and assorted colors, rubber cement, glue, glitter, scissors, yarn, pencil

Directions:

1. Cut two 8 ½" x 11" sheets of different colored tissue paper. Cover one sheet with rubber cement. Then carefully place the second sheet on top of the first one.

2. Fold the double, glued, colored tissue paper in half lengthwise.

3. Cut the tissue paper as indicated by the dotted lines in the illustration.

4. Unfold the "ladder." If you want, flip the layers over alternately to show the two colors better.

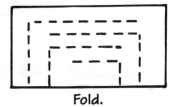

Fold.

5. Tie a piece of yarn to the smallest rectangle and hang up the ladder.

6. Use rubber cement to glue white and a light color of tissue paper together. Using the angel pattern, trace around and cut out as many angels as you wish. Decorate with glitter.

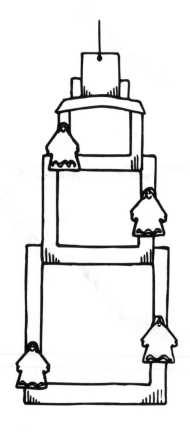

7. Glue your angels on the "ladder."

8. Let your "Jacob's ladder" remind you of the presence of God in your life.

Other Ideas:

1. Cut angels out of plain, white pieces of tissue paper.

2. Omit angels from the cutout ladder.

3. Stick tissue paper to clear adhesive plastic before cutting out the ladder and angels.

angel pattern

© Shining Star Publications

SS20001

The Lord is my shepherd . . .
(Psalm 23:1)

A Sheep for the Shepherd

Materials:

8" paper plate, white tagboard (optional), white tissue paper, glue, markers, scissors, patterns on page 50

Directions:

1. Cut out the patterns.

2. Color the words on the staff and the sheep's eye.

3. Glue the ear to the sheep's head. Then glue the pattern pieces on the paper plate. The head and feet go on the front of the plate; the staff pieces go behind it.

4. Cut white tissue paper into 3" x 3" pieces, crumple them into balls, and glue them on the paper plate for sheep's wool.

5. Let the sheep remind you that Jesus, your loving shepherd, is always watching over you.

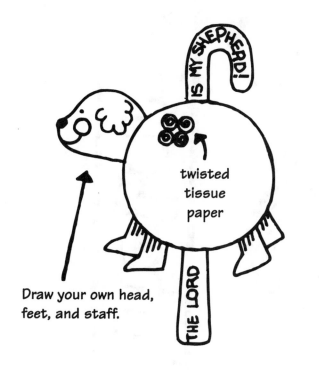

twisted tissue paper

Draw your own head, feet, and staff.

Other Ideas:

1. For more durability, glue the patterns onto tagboard.

2. Omit the staff.

3. Draw the head, feet, and staff on construction paper instead of using the patterns.

4. Twist squares of tissue paper around a pencil before gluing them on.

© Shining Star Publications

49

SS20001

Patterns

back feet

head

front feet

ear

my shepherd!

The Lord is

staff

© Shining Star Publications

SS20001

*. . . and they brought Daniel and
threw him into the lions' den . . .*
(Daniel 6:16)

Puppet Fun With Daniel

Materials:

tissue paper in assorted colors,
posterboard, markers or crayons,
scissors, white glue and water in equal
parts, sponge brush, toilet paper or
paper towel tube (5" x 1¾"), patterns
on page 52

Directions:

1. Cut out the patterns.

2. Trace around the patterns on
   posterboard and cut them out.

3. Tear or cut pieces of colored tissue
   paper for Daniel's robe and the
   lion's body. Brush on the glue and
   water mixture and paste the
   pieces in place. Cover with another layer of glue and water. Let dry.

4. Use markers to color the heads of Daniel and the lion. Then glue them to their bodies.

5. Cut strips of tissue paper and glue them on Daniel for hair and a beard. Do the same
   for the lion's mane. If desired, curl the strips around a pencil before gluing them in
   place.

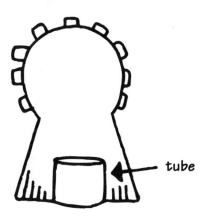

tube

6. Cut the cardboard tube into two 2½" x 1¾"
   parts. Glue one tube segment to the back of
   each puppet piece at the bottom.

7. Stand up the figures and use them to act out
   the story of "Daniel in the Lions' Den."

Other Ideas:

1. Add more puppets for the king, the angel, and
   additional lions.

2. Draw your own puppet patterns.

3. Add facial features made from tissue paper.

© Shining Star Publications

SS20001

Patterns

Glue head here.

Glue head here.

© Shining Star Publications

. . . So he set a royal crown on her head and made her queen . . .
(Esther 2:17)

A Crown for the Queen

Materials:

tissue paper in assorted colors, colored construction paper, scissors, white glue, yarn, tape, pencil, patterns on page 54

Directions:

1. Trace around the patterns on a piece of construction paper. Cut them out and tape them end to end. (A third piece can be added to make the crown larger.)

2. Cut pieces of yarn and glue them on the construction paper crown.

3. Cut 3" x 3" pieces of colored tissue paper, crumple them into balls, and glue them on the crown.

4. Size the crown to your head and tape it together at the back.

5. Pretend to be Queen Esther, telling the story of how God used you to save His people.

Other Ideas:

1. Make a crushed tissue paper crown to use with other stories of Bible kings and queens.

2. Glue uncrumpled, 1½" x 1½" tissue paper squares on the crown.

3. Add glitter as desired.

4. Omit yarn and use only tissue paper.

5. Cut 1" x 12" strips of tissue paper and wrap them around pieces of yarn or string to make tissue cord. Glue the tissue cord on the crown.

6. Write "I'm a Queen (or King) in God's Kingdom" around the crown. Talk about how each of us, like Esther, has a job to do in helping others.

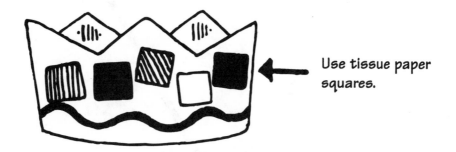

Use tissue paper squares.

© Shining Star Publications

SS20001

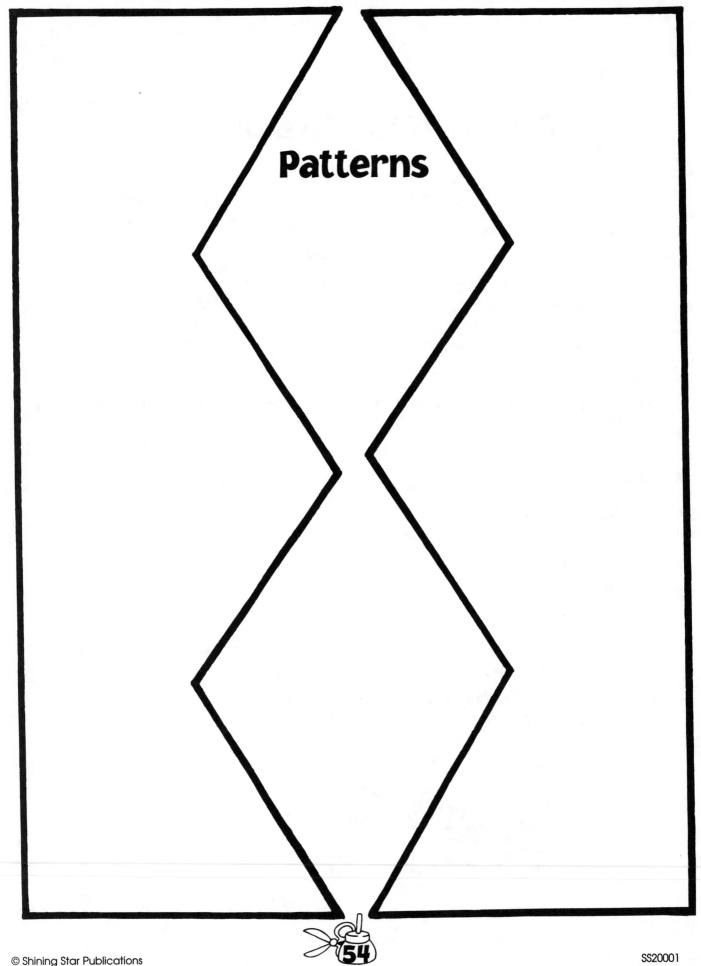

Patterns

© Shining Star Publications

SS20001

Then an angel of the Lord appeared to him (Zechariah) . . .
(Luke 1:11)

Jesus Is the Reason Wreath

Jesus is the Reason for the Season.

Materials:

red and green tissue paper, paper plate, tagboard, white glue, pencil with eraser, scissors, markers or crayons, patterns on page 56

Directions:

1. Cut out the patterns.

2. Use markers or crayons to color the words inside the circle.

3. Glue the circle pattern to the center of a paper plate.

4. Trace around the bow pattern on a piece of tagboard. Cut it out and glue it to the bottom of the paper plate.

5. Cut 3" x 3" squares of green and red tissue paper.

6. Hold a pencil, eraser end down, in the middle of each square and twist the tissue paper around it.

7. Glue green tissue paper squares to the wreath and red tissue paper squares to the bow.

8. John the Baptist helped people get ready for Jesus. Let the wreath help you get ready for Christmas by remembering that Jesus is the real reason for the Christmas season.

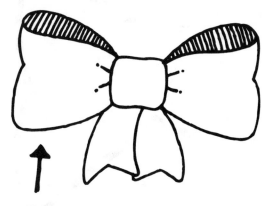

Use a
real bow.

Other Ideas:

1. Glue squares of flat tissue paper directly to the wreath.

2. Crumple squares of tissue paper instead of twisting them.

3. Cut out the center of the paper plate and omit the pattern piece.

4. Use a real bow instead of the tissue one.

5. Cover a large tagboard wreath as a class project.

© Shining Star Publications

55

SS20001

Patterns

Jesus
is the
Reason
for the
Season.

56

© Shining Star Publications

SS20001

. . . "Do not be afraid, Mary . . . You will . . . give birth to a son, and you are to give him the name Jesus."
(Luke 1:30–31)

Christmas Angel

Materials:
tissue paper in light colors, paper doilies, pencil, rubber cement, glue, hole punch, scissors, patterns on page 58

Directions:
1. Cut out the patterns.

2. Cut tissue paper to fit over the angel's wings and body; glue it on with rubber cement. (Or, use a mixture of equal parts of white glue and water.)

3. Cut pieces of paper doilies to fit over the angel's body and wings. Glue the pieces over the tissue paper.

4. Shape the body of the angel into a cone and glue.

5. Glue the wings to the back of the angel.

6. Use a hole punch to make tissue eyes and a mouth for the angel; glue them on with rubber cement.

7. Cut strips of tissue paper (½" x 4"), wrap them around a pencil to curl, and glue them on the angel for hair.

8. Use the angel as a puppet to tell different parts of the Christmas story. Then put it on top of a Christmas tree.

Other Ideas:
1. Write "Joy" with tissue paper pieces and paste them on the angel.

2. Cut and glue small pieces of tissue paper and paper doilies over the angel. Add glitter and sequins as desired.

3. Cut the patterns out of tagboard and staple them together.

Try glitter and sequins.

© Shining Star Publications

SS20001

Patterns

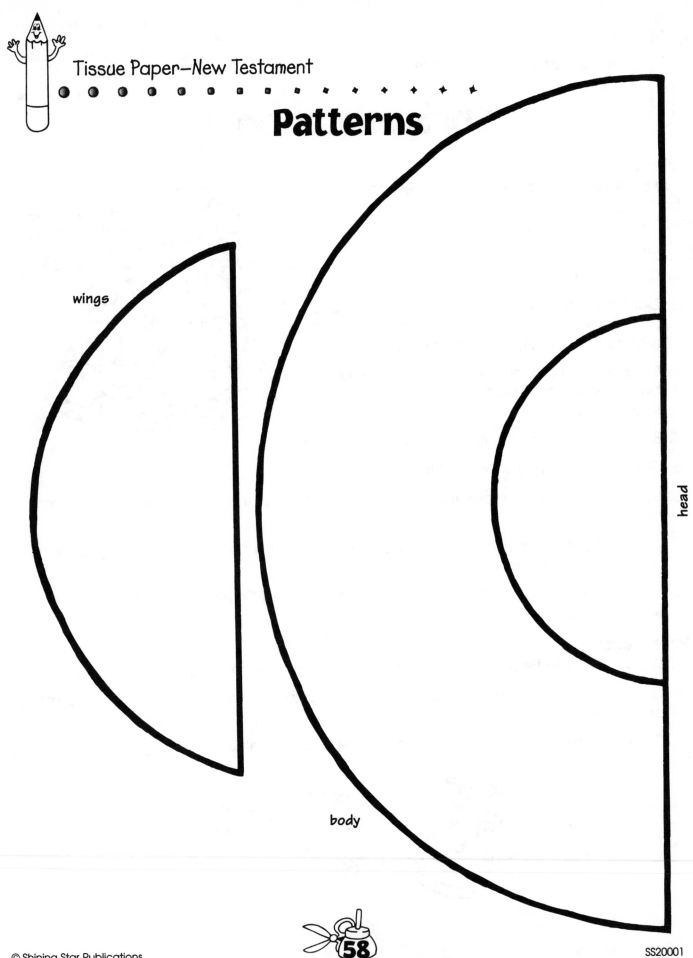

wings

head

body

© Shining Star Publications

SS20001

Tissue Paper—New Testament

and she gave birth to her firstborn, a son. She wrapped him in cloths and placed him in a manger . . .

(Luke 2:7)

Nativity Mobile

Materials:

tissue paper in assorted colors, black construction paper, yarn, hole punch, scissors, pencil, white glue, patterns on page 60

Directions:

1. Cut out the patterns. Cut out the inside of the patterns as well as the outside.

2. Trace around the patterns on black construction paper. Cut them out. Don't forget to cut out the insides.

3. Trace the inside sections of the patterns on colored tissue paper, allowing 1/2" space on all sides. Cut out the sections.

4. Glue the colored tissue pieces over the black construction paper pieces.

5. Punch holes in the black construction paper pieces as indicated.

6. Cut and tie pieces of yarn through the holes to connect the mobile pieces.

7. Hang your mobile to proclaim Jesus' birth.

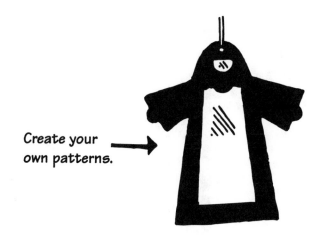

Create your own patterns.

Other Ideas:

1. For more durability, cut the shapes for the mobile from tagboard.

2. Draw and cut out your own patterns for a Christmas mobile.

3. Cover the mobile outlines with clear adhesive plastic. Then fill the inside sections with small pieces of tissue paper. Cover with a second piece of adhesive plastic when finished.

© Shining Star Publications

SS20001

Patterns

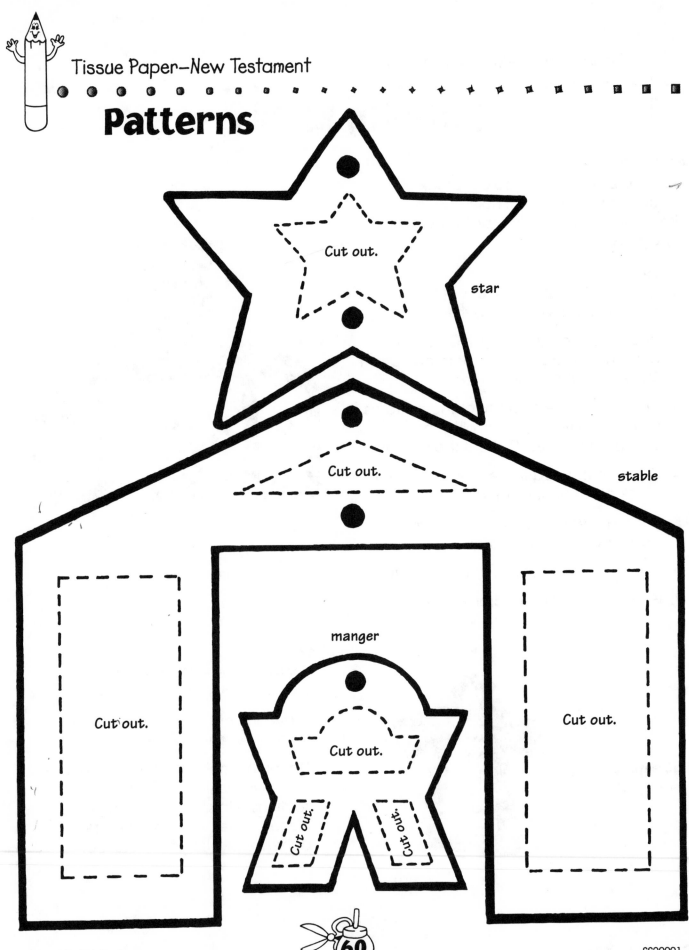

star

Cut out.

stable

Cut out.

manger

Cut out.

Cut out.

Cut out.

Cut out.

Cut out.

Cut out.

© Shining Star Publications

60

SS20001

. . . "Do not be afraid. I bring you good news of great joy that will be for all the people." (Luke 2:10)

Glory in the Highest Windsock

Materials:

white and yellow tissue paper
white paper (optional)
white tagboard
pencil
paper towel or toilet paper tube (4 ½" x 1 ¾")
yarn
markers
hole punch
scissors
ruler
rubber cement
white glue
paper doily
pattern on page 62

Directions:

1. Cut out the wings pattern. Trace around the wings pattern on a piece of white tagboard and cut it out.

2. Trace around the wings pattern on the paper doily. Cut it out and attach it to the tagboard wings using white glue.

3. If the tube is not white, cover it with a strip of white paper.

4. Cut a 6" x 7 ½" strip of white tissue paper.

5. Cut fringe, 1" wide and 1 ½" in length, along the width of the tissue paper strip.

6. Use rubber cement (or white glue and water) to attach the tissue paper strip to the side of the tube, 1 ¼" from the top, leaving the fringe hanging free at the bottom.

7. Use markers to draw facial features on the top of the tube for the angel's face.

8. Cut out strips of yellow tissue paper for hair and glue them around the angel's face.

9. Use white glue to attach the wings to the back of the angel.

10. Punch holes on opposite sides of the angel. Cut a piece of yarn and tie it through the holes for a hanger.

11. Hang the angel windsock as a reminder of the angel that appeared to the shepherds on the first Christmas night.

© Shining Star Publications

SS20001

Glory in the Highest
Windsock continued

Other Ideas:

1. Cut the paper doily into small pieces and glue them to the wings.

2. Glue aluminum foil or lightly colored tissue paper to the wings under the paper doily pieces.

3. Omit the paper doily.

4. Add glitter.

5. Instead of drawing the face, use a hole punch to make tissue paper circles to glue on for the angel's eyes and mouth.

6. Curl the tissue paper strips around a pencil before attaching them to make the angel's hair.

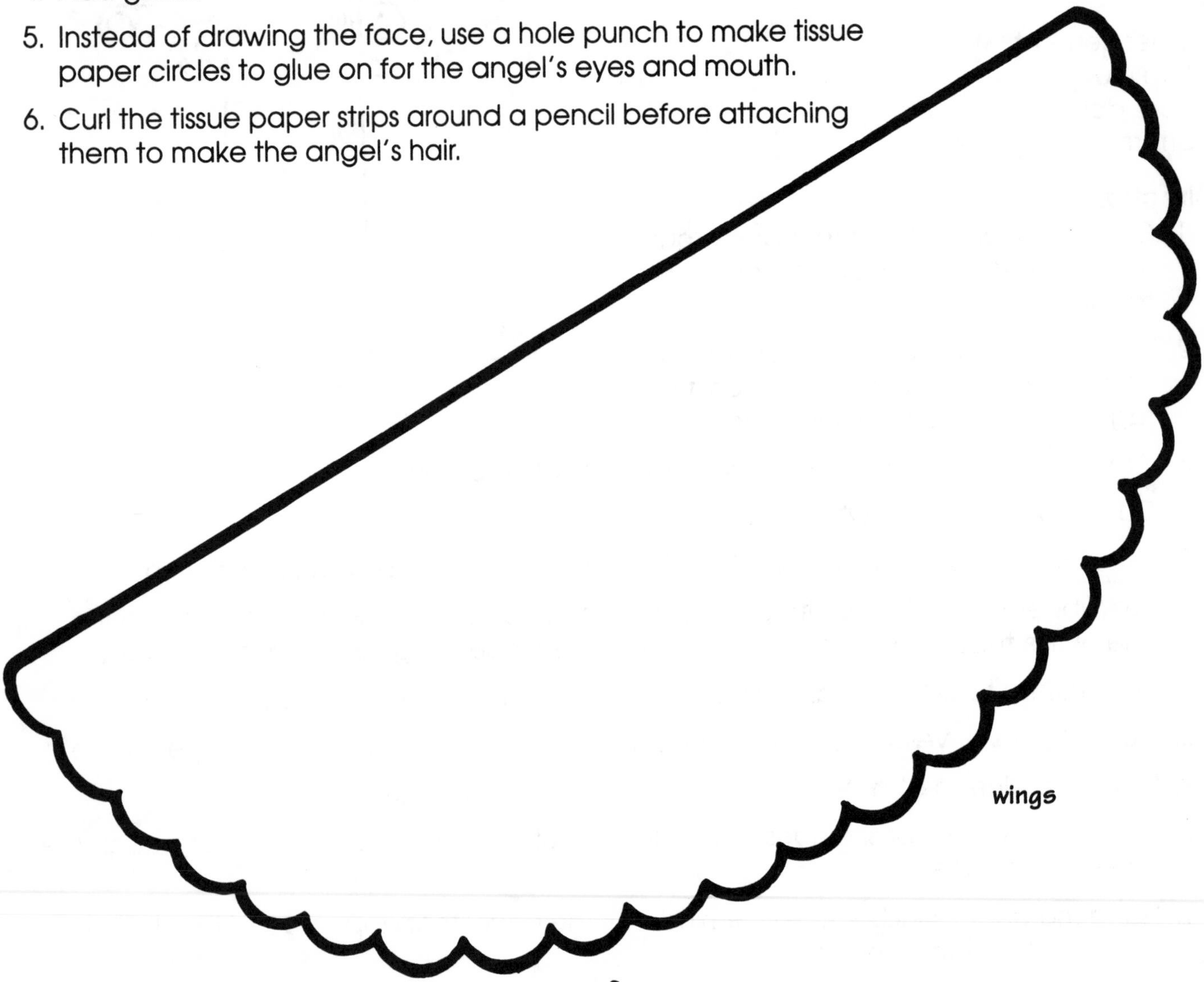

wings

62

© Shining Star Publications

SS20001

The shepherds returned, glorifying and praising God for all the things they had heard and seen . . . (Luke 2:20)

Spread the Good News Ornament

Materials:

colored tissue paper, yarn, white glue and water in equal parts, Styrofoam™ tray, scissors, pencil, pattern below

Directions:

1. Dip yarn in the glue and water mixture until wet. Arrange the wet yarn in a bell shape on the Styrofoam™ tray. If you wish, use the outline at the bottom of this page for a bell pattern.

2. Add more wet yarn to the bell, making sure to touch the sides often. Let the yarn dry. Remove the yarn bell from the Styrofoam™ tray.

3. Tie a loop of yarn at the top of the bell.

4. Trace the bell shape on a piece of colored tissue paper. Cut out the shape ½" larger than the yarn bell.

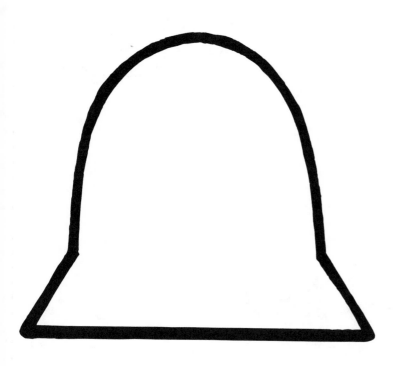

5. Glue the tissue paper bell to the yarn. Let it dry; then trim the excess edges.

6. Put the bell on the tree and remember to share the good news of Jesus' birth with others.

Other Ideas:

1. Use Christmas cookie cutter shapes for ornament outlines.

2. Draw your own Christmas ornament designs.

3. Use several colors of tissue paper for the bell.

© Shining Star Publications

63

SS20001

Tissue Paper–New Testament

From a Tiny Seed

Materials:

tissue paper in green, brown, and other assorted colors; white glue and water in equal parts; sponge brush; pencil; scissors; tagboard; mustard seed; paper towel or toilet paper tube (4½" x 1¾"); patterns on page 65

Directions:

1. Cut out the patterns.

2. Trace around the treetop pattern on a piece of tagboard.

3. Cut eight or more 4" x 3" pieces of green tissue paper, and fringe them. Overlap and glue these tissue pieces on the treetop pattern.

4. Use colored tissue paper to trace around and cut out birds and nests using the patterns. If desired, fringe the birds' tails. Glue the birds on the tree.

5. Cut or tear small pieces of brown tissue paper and glue them on the cardboard tube.

6. Cut two 1" slits, opposite each other, in one end of the tube.

7. Slip the treetop into the slits to make it stand.

8. Glue a mustard seed (or other small seed) at the bottom of the tree trunk.

9. Read Jesus' words about how the kingdom of heaven is like a plant that started as a tiny seed and then grew into a big tree where birds make their nests. (Luke 13:18–19) Talk about ways you can help God's kingdom grow.

Other Ideas:

1. Glue crumpled tissue paper on the tree.

2. Cut out the birds from colored construction paper. Add feathers if desired.

3. Use the tree to illustrate the tree planted by the water in Psalm 1:3.

© Shining Star Publications

SS20001

Patterns

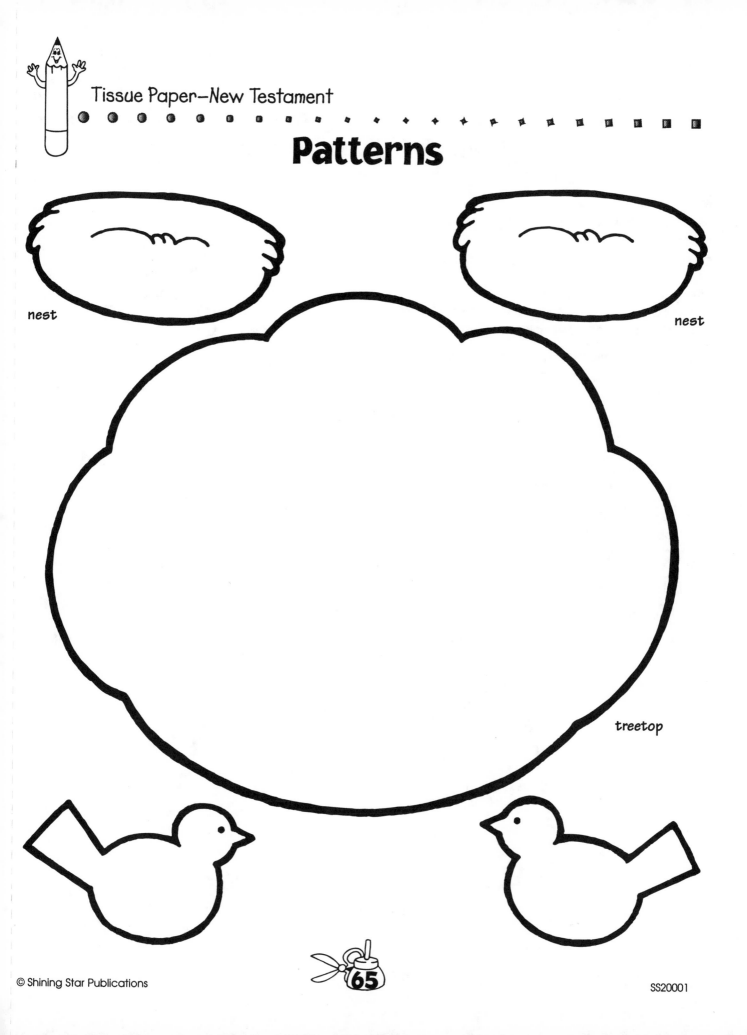

nest

nest

treetop

*"Come, follow me," Jesus said, "and
I will make you fishers of men."*
(Matthew 4:19)

Caught by Jesus

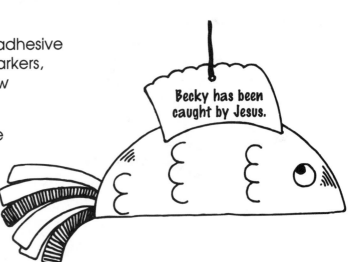

Materials:

tissue paper in assorted colors, plate, clear adhesive
plastic, pencil, scissors, hole punch, yarn, markers,
construction paper, stapler, fin pattern below

Directions:

1. Use a plate to trace a circle on a piece
   of clear adhesive plastic. Cut it out.

2. Cut half circles out of tissue paper
   for scales and one full circle for
   an eye.

3. Cut streamers out of tissue paper for
   a tail.

4. Cut out the fin pattern. Trace around the fin on a piece of construction paper. Write on
   it *"(Your name) has been caught by Jesus."*

5. Take the paper backing off the circle of adhesive plastic. Working on half of the fish,
   put on the tissue eye, scales, and tail. Add the fin to the top of the fish.

6. Fold the bottom half of the circle over the top half.

7. Staple the fin in place for more stability.

8. Punch a hole in the top of the fin and put a piece of yarn through it.

9. Hang the fish as a reminder that Jesus has "caught" you to spread His love to others.

fin

© Shining Star Publications

SS20001

"... 'Our Father in heaven,
hallowed be your name.'"
(Matthew 6:9)

Pray to the Lord Sun Catcher

Materials:

tissue paper, rubber cement, plate, scissors,
construction paper, yarn, pencil, markers, ruler

Directions:

1. Use a plate to trace a circle on both the tissue
   paper and construction paper. Cut them out.

2. Measure a second circle on the construction
   paper, 1" inside the first one. Cut out and keep
   the smaller circle, leaving a 1" rim for the
   outside of the sun catcher.

3. Write "Pray to the Lord." around the 1" rim.

4. On the cutout circle of construction paper,
   outline your hand, fingers together, and cut
   it out.

5. Use rubber cement to glue the circle of colored
   tissue paper on the back of the sun catcher rim. Glue
   your handprint outline on the center of the tissue paper.

6. Punch a hole at the top of the rim and tie a piece of yarn through it.

7. Put up your sun catcher to remind you to pray to the Lord.

Other Ideas:

1. Cover each side of the sun catcher with a piece of clear adhesive plastic.

2. Cut the hand shape out of tissue paper.

3. Use different colored tissue on clear adhesive plastic, add the hands, and finish off
   with a glue-and-water wash.

4. Draw your own design for the sun catcher.

Try a heart design in
your sun catcher.

© Shining Star Publications

SS20001

But seek first his kingdom and his righteousness, and all these things will be given to you as well.
(Matthew 6:33)

God Cares for You

Tissue Flowers

Materials:

tissue paper in assorted colors, green florist tape, scissors, pipe cleaners, construction paper in light colors, markers or crayons, juice container, yardstick, glue

Directions:

1. Cut tissue paper into 6" x 20" strips.

2. Fold each strip in half lengthwise.

3. Roll the strip around the end of a pipe cleaner to make a flower, gathering the unfolded tissue edges together as you work.

4. Tape the base of the flower to the pipe cleaner with green florist tape.

5. Make more flowers using these directions or one of the sets of directions on pages 69–70, adjusting the width of the flower to the size desired.

© Shining Star Publications

SS20001

God Cares for You continued

Yardstick Flowers

Directions:

1. Cut tissue paper into 6" x 20" strips.

2. Fold each strip in half lengthwise.

3. Place the yardstick inside the folded tissue, even with the fold.

4. Crinkle the tissue by pushing it together along the top of the yardstick.

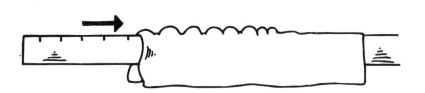

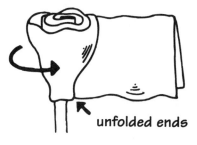

unfolded ends

5. Take the tissue off the yardstick.

6. Roll the strip around the end of a pipe cleaner to make a flower, gathering the unfolded tissue edge together as you work.

7. Tape the base of the flower to the pipe cleaner with green florist tape.

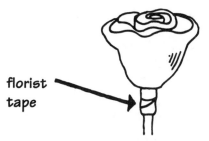

florist tape

© Shining Star Publications

SS20001

God Cares for You continued

Flowers With Petals

Directions:

1. Cut tissue into 3" x 20" strips.

2. Cut petal shapes into the unfolded edges of the strip. If needed, duplicate the petal pattern below.

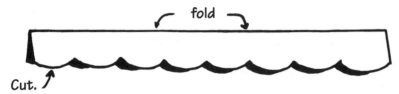

fold

Cut.

3. Roll the strip around the end of a pipe cleaner to make a flower, gathering the folded tissue edge together as you work.

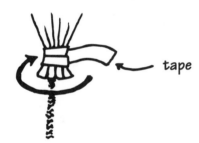

tape

4. Tape the base of the flower to the pipe cleaner with green florist tape.

Flower Vase:

1. Cut a piece of light-colored construction paper to fit around a juice container.

2. Write "God Cares for You!" on the paper.

3. Glue the paper around the juice container.

4. Place the flowers inside the vase you have made.

5. As you look at the flowers, remember that God, who cares for every flower that grows, also cares for you.

Other Ideas:

1. Decorate your juice container vase with cutout tissue flowers or scrap tissue pieces.

2. Crumple a strip of tissue paper over a round dowel instead of a yardstick.

© Shining Star Publications

SS20001

Tissue Paper—New Testament

Put Your Trust in the Lord Bookmark

Put Your Trust

in the Lord.

Materials:

tissue paper in assorted colors; clear adhesive plastic; pressed, dried flowers and leaves; construction paper; scissors; ruler; pencil; markers; newspaper; phone book

Directions:

1. Press flowers and leaves by placing them between newspaper sheets and slipping them inside a large phone book for a week until their moisture is removed.

2. Cut construction paper into a 2" x 6" rectangle. Cut out the middle of the rectangle leaving a ⅜" border (frame).

   Cut out.

3. Cut out two 2" x 6" pieces of clear adhesive plastic.

4. Print "Put Your Trust in the Lord." around the frame, adding decorations as desired.

5. Cut small pieces of colored tissue paper.

6. Remove the backing from one piece of clear adhesive plastic.

7. Place the frame, printed side down, on the plastic.

8. Add pieces of colored tissue paper, as well as dried flowers and leaves.

9. Cover with the other piece of clear adhesive plastic.

10. Let the bookmark remind you to trust in God to take care of you.

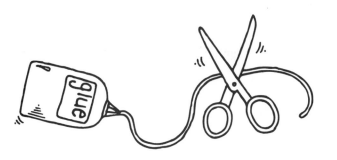

Other Ideas:

1. Cut out the frame from tissue paper.

2. Brush a mixture of white glue and water over the pressed flowers and cover with white or light-colored tissue paper.

3. Write a Bible verse of your choice on the bookmark frame.

© Shining Star Publications

SS20001

. . . Love each other. (John 15:17)

Love One Another Banner

Materials:
tissue paper in assorted colors
white paper
rubber cement (or white glue
    and water mixture)
glue
brush
markers
scissors
pencil
straw
yarn
patterns on page 73

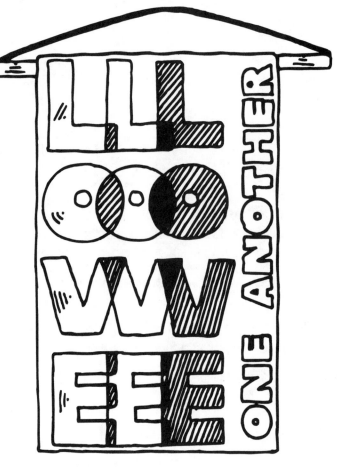

Directions:
1. Cut out the patterns for the banner and letters.

2. Trace around the banner on white paper and cut it out. Trace around each letter on colored tissue paper three times and cut them out.

3. Use rubber cement to glue the letter *L* at the top left side of the banner below the dotted line. Overlap and glue down the other *L*s beside it.

4. Place the letter *O* below the *L* and glue it down. Add the duplicate letter *O*s. Repeat with the *V*s and *E*s. (See the illustration.)

5. Use markers to color the words "one another" along the right side of the banner.

6. Fold the banner on the dotted line and glue the top over a straw. Tie a piece of yarn to each end of the straw.

7. Hang the banner and read John 15:17 in your Bible. Talk about ways you can show love to others.

Other Ideas:
1. Add overlapped heart shapes to the banner.

2. Overlap letters or symbols to illustrate other Bible stories.

© Shining Star Publications

SS20001

Patterns

L O V E

ONE ANOTHER

Fold.

73

© Shining Star Publications

SS20001

. . . they met a man from Cyrene, named Simon, and they forced him to carry the cross.
(Matthew 27:32)

Calvary's Stained-Glass Cross Window

Materials:

tissue paper in assorted colors, black construction paper, scissors, glue, hole punch, yarn, pattern on page 75

Directions:

1. Cut out the window pattern.

2. Trace around the pattern on black construction paper and cut it out. Don't forget to cut out all the dotted areas.

3. Cut pieces of colored tissue paper to fit over the holes in the window, allowing about ⅜" extra on all sides. Use the same or related colors for all holes that help make up the cross shape.

4. Fit and glue the cut pieces of colored tissue paper in place on the back of the window.

5. Punch a hole at the top of the window and tie a piece of yarn through it.

6. Let the window remind you that Jesus died to give you eternal life.

Other Ideas:

1. Draw your own cross and frame to fill in with tissue paper.

2. Make a stained-glass window to go with another Bible story.

3. Cover the window with two pieces of clear adhesive plastic.

Make your own cross.

Illustrate another Bible story (for example, "Jonah and the Big Fish").

© Shining Star Publications

74

SS20001

Pattern

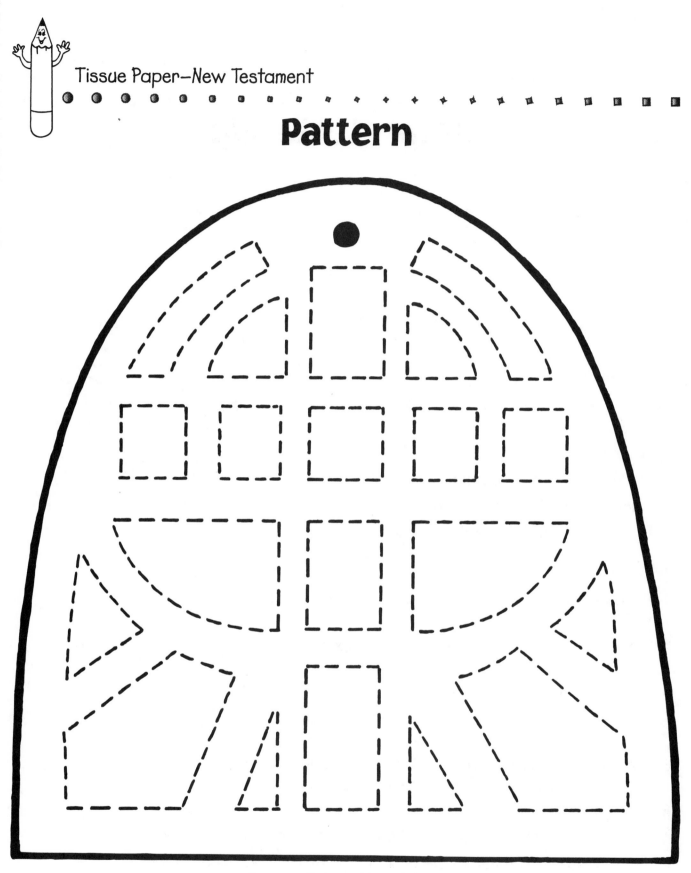

Cut out all dotted line shapes.

© Shining Star Publications

75

SS20001

"He is not here; he has risen . . ."
(Matthew 28:6)

Easter Butterfly

Materials:

white tissue paper
construction paper
pencil
scissors
food coloring
eyedropper
water
small containers for water
glue
newspaper
hole punch
yarn
pattern on page 77

Directions:

1. Cut out the butterfly pattern.

2. Trace around the outside rim of the butterfly on a piece of construction paper. Cut it out.

3. Trace the inside butterfly pattern on a piece of white tissue paper. Cut it out.

4. Put a few drops of food coloring into containers of water, using as many colors as you wish.

5. Place the white tissue paper on the newspaper. Use the eyedropper to drop food coloring onto the white tissue paper. Let dry.

6. Glue the tissue paper to the construction paper butterfly.

7. Punch a hole in the top of each side of the butterfly. Tie a piece of yarn through the holes.

8. A butterfly comes from a dead-looking cocoon, just like Jesus came out of the grave. Let your butterfly remind you to be happy that Jesus is alive.

Other Ideas:

1. Make flowers or wrapping paper from tissue paper you have colored.

2. Draw your own butterfly shape to fill in with the colored tissue paper.

3. Make and cut out colored tissue shapes to illustrate other Bible stories.

© Shining Star Publications

SS20001

Pattern

© Shining Star Publications

SS20001

Tissue Paper—New Testament

*". . . This same Jesus . . .
will come back . . ."*
(Acts 1:11)

He Will Come Again

Materials:

tissue paper in assorted colors, sheet of clear heavy plastic, rubber cement (or white glue and water mixture), colored glue, scissors, pencil, hole punch, yarn, markers, pattern on page 79

Directions:

1. Cut out the window pattern.

2. Cut a piece of clear plastic to fit the window.

3. Trace and cut pattern shapes out of different colors of tissue paper to match the shapes in the window pattern.

4. Use rubber cement to attach the tissue shapes to the plastic.

5. Outline the shapes with colored glue.

6. Use markers to draw in Jesus' eyes, nose, and mouth.

7. Punch a hole in the top of the window and tie a piece of yarn for hanging.

8. Let your picture of Jesus remind you that though you cannot see Him, He is always with you.

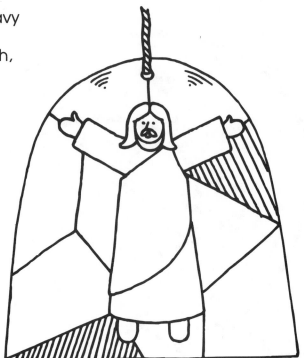

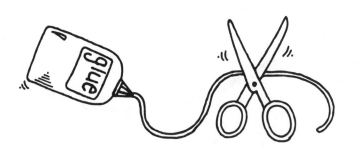

Other Ideas:

1. Place the tissue paper pieces between two sheets of clear adhesive plastic.

2. Use your own drawing of Jesus to make a "leaded" tissue window.

3. Omit the colored glue.

4. Cut a piece of black tissue paper or construction paper for the pieces to fit into.

© Shining Star Publications

78

SS20001

Pattern

© Shining Star Publications

SS20001

Simply Fancy Gift Bag

Give gifts to others to share God's love.
Put the gifts in these attractive bags.

Materials:
any size and color of paper bag
cookie cutters
stickers
crayons or markers
hole punch
scissors
string, ribbon, lace, or yarn
pencil

Directions:
1. Place the bag in a flat position on a table or desk.

2. If using a cookie cutter, trace around the outer edge of the shape (see illustration) on the bag.

3. With the crayons or markers, fill in faces and details on the cookie cutter shapes.

4. Stickers may be used with the cookie cutter designs or by themselves on the outside of the bag.

5. Fold down the top of the bag one time and punch two holes near the center.

6. Cut the appropriate size string, ribbon, lace, or yarn and thread it through the two holes. Leave the two ends on one side so they can be tied into a fancy bow.

Uses for the Gift Bag:
1. Use it for gifts on Mother's or Father's Day.

2. Use it at Christmas for gifts.

3. Fill it with treats to take to shut-ins, children in the hospital, etc.

4. Put a prize in it to use as a reward when someone does something special.

© Shining Star Publications

SS20001

Ring the Bell!

Materials:

very small bag, pencil, scissors, markers or crayons, drinking straw, tape, small gold or silver bell, yarn

Directions:

1. Fold a small bag into a flat position. Lightly mark the cutting lines with a pencil as shown in Figure 1.

2. Trim the top edge of the bag in a small arch shape (Figure 1).

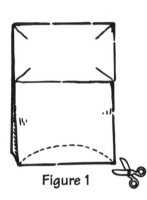

Figure 1

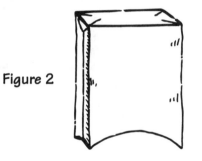

Figure 2

3. While the bag is flat, decorate it with markers or crayons.

4. Open the bag (Figure 2).

5. Cut a drinking straw in half. Thread a piece of yarn through it.

6. Tie one end of the yarn to a small bell. Knot the other end on the outside of the straw (Figure 3). Note: This should be done for younger children.

7. Punch a hole through the bottom center of the bag.

8. Push the straw (bell handle) through the hole, and tape it securely inside and outside the paper bag (Figure 3).

Uses for the Bell:

1. Use the bell for a Christmas decoration.

2. Ring bell while singing a song.

3. When studying about your church, use the bell to symbolize the church or the church bell.

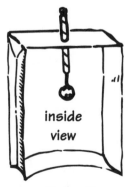

inside view

Figure 3

© Shining Star Publications

SS20001

Paper Bags

"This will be a sign to you: You will find a baby wrapped in cloths and lying in a manger."
(Luke 2:12)

Baby Cradle

Materials:
brown lunch bag
scissors
glue or tape
small fabric squares
baby pattern on page 83
crayons
straw or yarn (for baby Jesus' cradle)

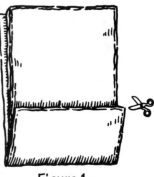

Directions:

1. Fold the bag flat. Using the bottom edge as a guide, cut off the top ¾ of the bag (Figure 1).

2. Fold the top half of the bottom of the bag to the inside and crease into place. This will give the cradle sturdier sides (Figure 2).

Figure 2

Figure 1

3. You may want to glue or tape the sides down to hold them in place (Figure 3).

4. Place straw or yarn in baby Jesus' cradle. (If making a cradle for another baby, use a fabric square instead of straw or yarn.)

5. Cut out the baby pattern.

Figure 3

6. Color the baby with crayons.

7. Place the baby in the cradle and cover him with a small fabric square for a blanket.

Uses for the Cradle:

1. Use it when telling the Christmas story or memorizing verses about Jesus' birth.

2. Use it to retell the stories of the birth of Isaac, Moses, Samuel, etc.

3. Use it as a prayer reminder. Write the name of a baby brother, sister, cousin, or friend on the back of the baby. Use it to help you remember to pray for that little one to grow to love Jesus.

82

© Shining Star Publications

SS20001

Pattern

© Shining Star Publications

SS20001

Church Designs

Materials:
large grocery bag, scissors, pencils, crayons or markers, Bible verse stickers (optional)

Directions:
1. Cut the bag apart. Start at the side seam and cut to the bottom, removing the bottom of the bag completely.

2. Fully open the bag and lay it flat.

3. Fold the sides of the bag to the center (Figure 1).

4. Mark the lines for the roof and cross shape; then cut on the lines (Figure 2).

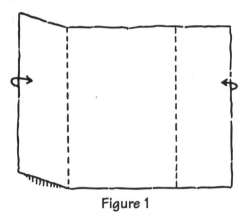

Figure 1

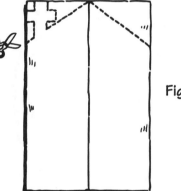

Figure 2

5. Open the church and draw pictures of the inside of your church. Color the church doors, stained-glass windows, etc.

6. Print a Bible verse about worship, prayer, or praise at the bottom on the inside or attach a preprinted Bible verse sticker.

Uses for the Church:
1. Use it to remind your family that they are part of the church, too.

2. After making the church, show it to a friend and have him or her tell why he or she likes to come to church.

3. Use it as an invitation to invite someone to come to a special service. Instead of drawing on the inside, glue a preprinted invitation to an upcoming meeting, party, or activity.

© Shining Star Publications

SS20001

A Beautiful Butterfly

Materials:
one 8" paper plate, scissors, crayons, glue, pattern below

Directions:

1. Cut the paper plate in half.

2. Cut out the wing pattern and trace it onto one of the plate halves. Reverse the pattern and trace it onto the other paper plate half. Cut them out. Glue the wings together as shown, overlapping about one inch.

3. Color using light colors. Then print "In Christ, We Are a New Creature." across the butterfly wings.

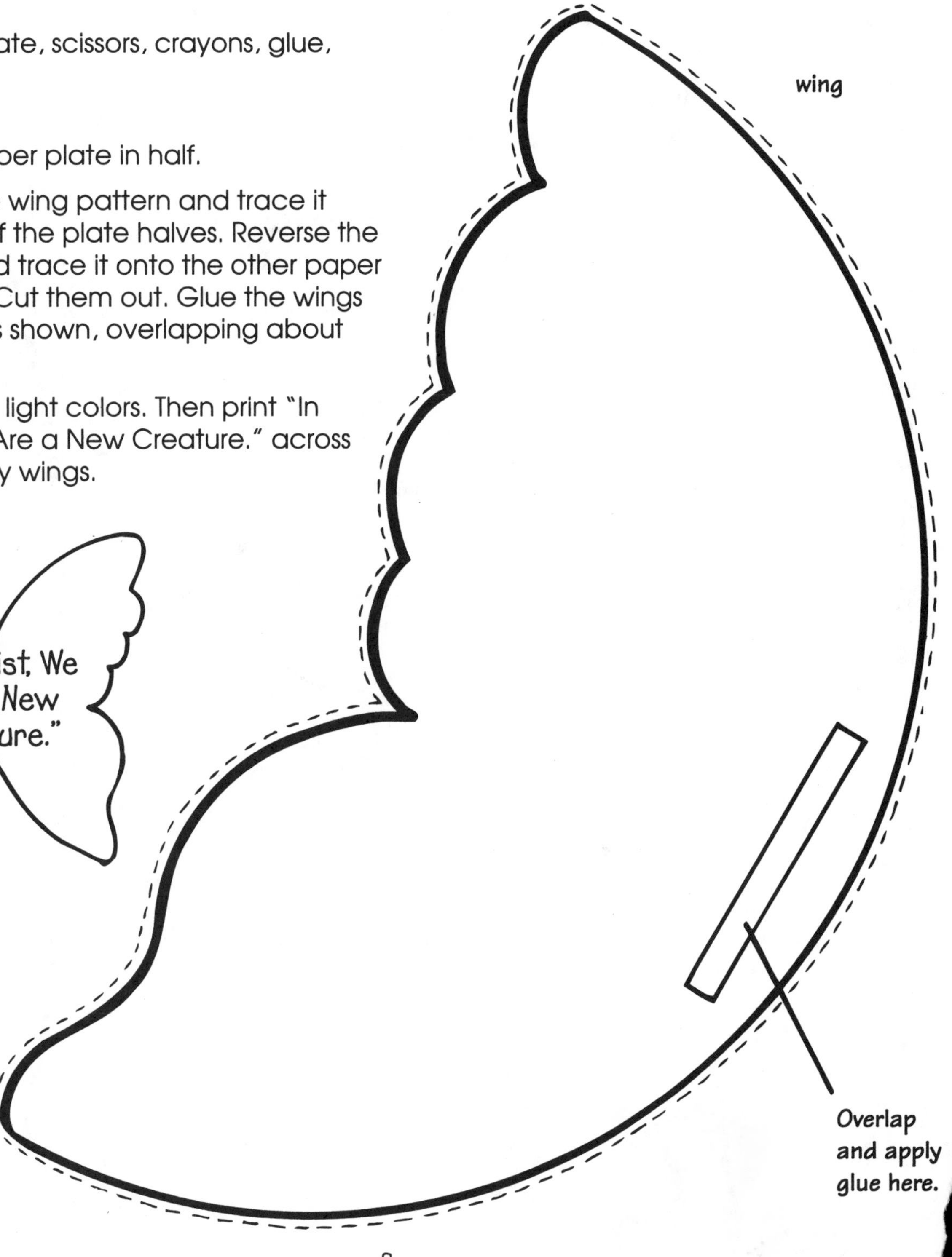

wing

"In Christ, We Are a New Creature."

Overlap and apply glue here.

24

© Shining Star Publications

SS2000

Patterns

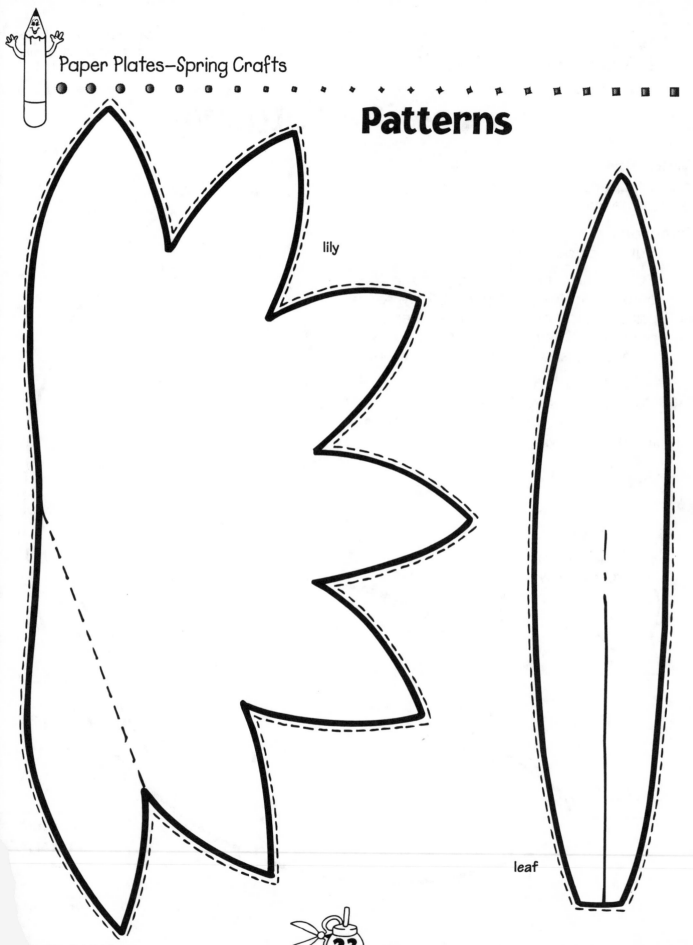

lily

leaf

23

Paper Bags

"Today in the town of David a Savior has been born to you; he is Christ the Lord." (Luke 2:11)

A "Bright" Nativity

Materials:

white lunch bag
patterns on pages 86–87
bright markers (crayons may be used but are not as brilliant in their reflection of light)
sand (1½" deep per bag)
votive candle
scissors
glue
ruler

Directions:

1. Cut out the patterns and color them.

2. Glue the patterns (one on the front and one on the back) to the paper bag. Only put glue around the outside of the patterns.

3. Cut off the top of the bag along the upper outline of the pattern. (See the finished project above.)

4. Fill the bag with 1½" of sand.

5. Ask an adult to help you set a votive candle deep in the sand in the center of the bag. The sand will keep the bag open and anchor the light.

Uses for the Nativity:

1. It can be an attractive centerpiece for a seasonal party (used at church or at home).

2. Use it as a verse reminder. Write a Bible verse on one side of the bag.

3. Use it to tell someone that Jesus is the Light of the World.

© Shining Star Publications

SS20001

© Shining Star Publications

Paper Bags

Pattern

front view

SS20001

Pattern

back view

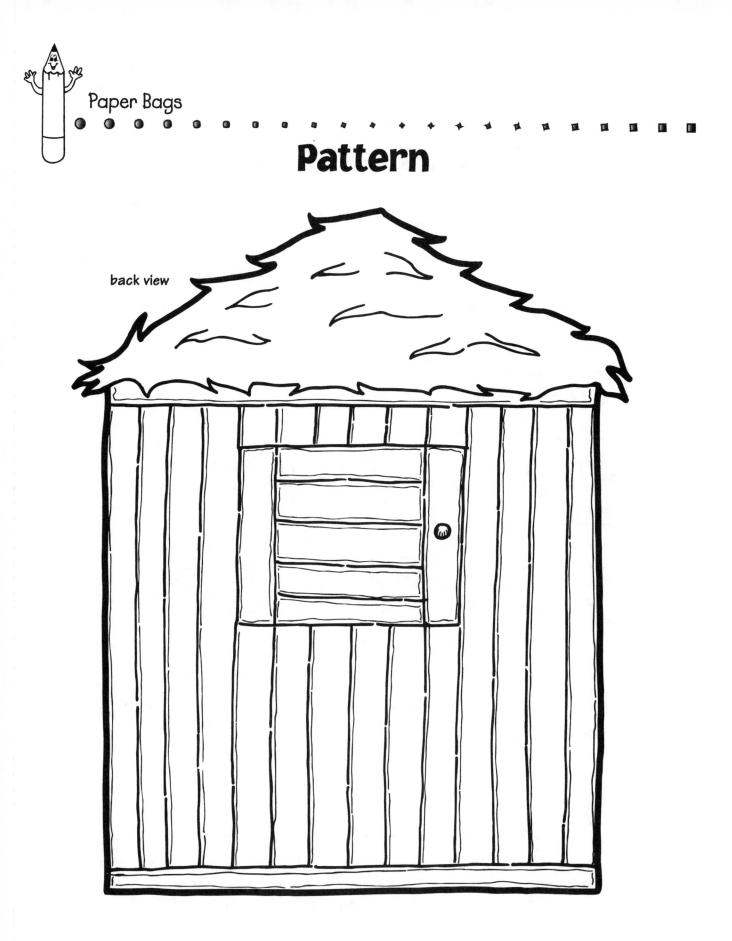

© Shining Star Publications

SS20001

"When my glory passes by, I will put you in a cleft in the rock and cover you with my hand . . ."
(Exodus 33:22)

Classy Book Cover

Materials:

large paper shopping bag; scissors; stickers, stamps, ink pads, and other decorative items; crayons; pencil

Directions:

1. Cut apart the bag, creating a flat rectangular piece that is larger than the book you wish to cover.

2. Decorate the cover with stickers, stamps, crayons, etc. (Figure 1).

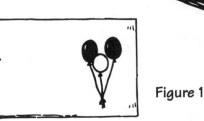

Figure 1

Figure 2

3. Open the book you wish to cover and lay it on the undecorated side of the paper bag (Figure 2).

4. Mark the place where you will need to make the fold at the top and bottom edges. Fold on the fold lines (Figure 3).

Figure 3

Figure 4

5. Close the book and pull the cover around it.

6. Open the book slightly and fold the paper cover over the book's hard cover (Figure 4).

7. Carefully slip the folded "slipcase" around the book's cover.

Uses for the Cover:

1. Print Bible verses on the cover and use it as a memory reminder.

2. Decorate it with seasonal stickers and stamps: winter—snowflake, Christmas motif; spring—flowers, raindrops, hearts, Easter motif; summer—billowy clouds, flowers, sunny shapes, fruits; autumn—leaves, pumpkins, vegetables, Thanksgiving motif.

© Shining Star Publications

SS20001

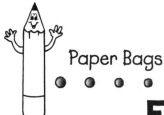

God made . . . all the creatures that move along the ground . . . And God saw that it was good. (Genesis 1:25)

Furry Creature Basket

Materials:
brown or white lunch bag
pencils
scissors
glue or tape
pattern of your choice on pages 90–91
crayons or markers
bristles from a paintbrush or other
   "whisker-type" items
cotton balls

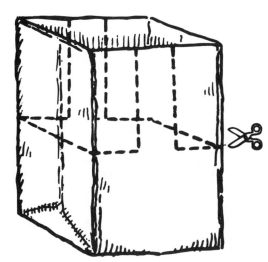

Directions:
1. Unfold a bag and lightly mark with a pencil the cutting lines on the sides (see illustration to the left).

2. Cut on the marked cutting lines.

3. Tape or glue the handle pieces together at the top.

4. Color and cut out one animal face.

5. Glue the face on one end of the basket; then attach whiskers, a tail, a fuzzy nose, etc.

Uses for the Basket:
1. Make the basket for a table decoration to be used at a party. Fill it with little treats, balloons, or other party favors.

2. On the side of the basket, print a Bible verse about God's love for His creatures. Use this for a memory reminder.

3. Place a small gift or several treats in the basket and give it away to brighten someone's day!

© Shining Star Publications

SS20001

Patterns

© Shining Star Publications

SS20001

Patterns

© Shining Star Publications

SS20001

Paper Bags

Bible Memory Place Cards

Materials:
small paper bags; scissors; tape; markers or pens; crayons; stickers, stamps, ink pads, and other decorative items; ruler

Directions:

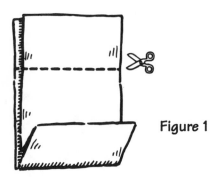

Figure 1

1. Measure down from the top of the bag about 4"–5" and draw a cutting line (Figure 1).

2. Cut on the cutting line.

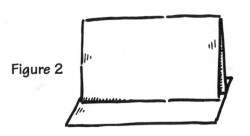

Figure 2

3. Fold down the bottom of the bag to form a stand; then fold over the top of the bag so that it connects evenly with the base of the bag (Figure 2).

4. Tape the folded portion down. This becomes the back side of the place card.

5. Print a memory verse on the place card and decorate it with crayons, stickers, or other decorative items.

6. Make several place cards.

"Blessed are the pure in heart, for they will see God."

Matthew 5:8

Uses for the Place Cards:

1. Use it as a memory verse reminder.

2. Print names on the cards when having a party.

3. Print your favorite Bible passage for a specific theme, such as love, trust, or kindness.

92

© Shining Star Publications

SS20001

She opens her arms to the poor and extends her hands to the needy. Her children arise and call her blessed . . .
(Proverbs 31:20, 28)

"Fan"ciful Mother's Day Present

Materials:

large, flat shopping bag (floral design if possible)
scissors
lace (18" per fan, depending on the size of the bag)
ruler
pencil
paper clip
ribbon (14" per fan)
glue

Directions:

1. Cut the nonseamed side of the flattened bag so that you have a large rectangular piece (Figure 1).

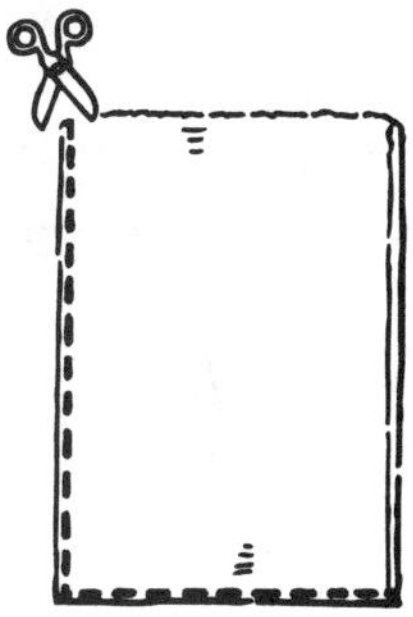

   Figure 1

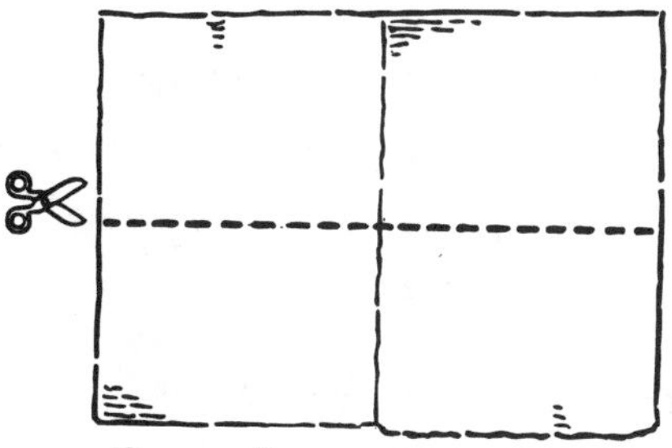

2. Fold the rectangular piece in half lengthwise and cut on the fold line. This will enable you to make two fans from the same bag (Figure 2).

   Figure 2

3. Glue lace along the long edge (Figure 3).

   Figure 3

4. Measure and mark every ½" for fold lines.

5. Beginning at one end, fold the paper into ½" accordion pleats (Figure 4).

   Figure 4

6. Apply a thin line of glue on the bottom edge of the folded paper, then hold the glued pleats together with a paper clip (Figure 5).

7. After the glue dries, fan the pleats out as far as possible.

8. Remove the paper clip and fold the corner upward to form two triangular shapes (Figure 6).

9. Add a small dab of glue to the folded corners. Wrap the ribbon around the end and tie it in place.

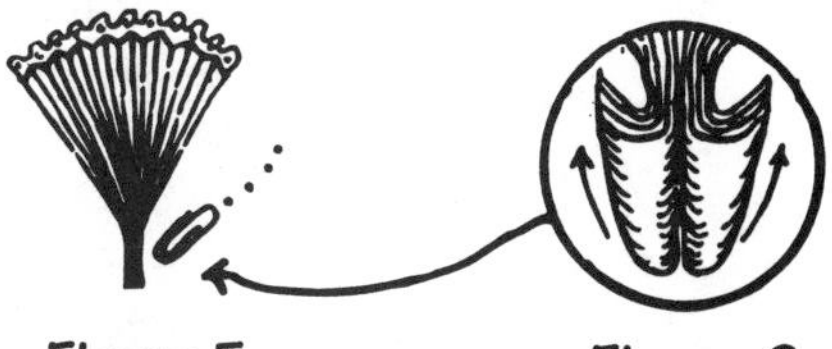

Figure 5   **Figure 6**

Uses for the Fan:

1. Make a fan to give as a Mother's Day gift.

2. At Christmastime, use a red or green bag to make a fan for a decoration or gift tag.

3. When discussing missions in Japan, make the fan and hang it in the classroom.

© Shining Star Publications   SS20001

Angel Decoration

God used an angel to announce the most important event ever—the birth of His Son!

Materials:
lunch bag
scissors
pattern on page 95
Styrofoam™ ball
yarn
glue
fine-line markers
lace (optional)

Directions:

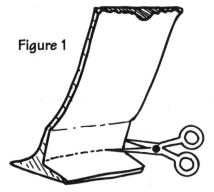

Figure 1

1. Remove the bottom rectangular piece from the flattened bag by cutting through all layers at the fold line (Figure 1).

2. Open the bag and twist the cut end to form the body of the angel (see the finished illustration above).

3. Cut out the arms pattern and glue it to the back of the bag.

4. Draw facial features on the Styrofoam™ ball (Figure 2).

5. Cut yarn for hair and glue it on the Styrofoam™ ball (Figure 3).

6. Glue the Styrofoam™ head to the paper bag body.

7. Optional: Glue lace around the neck of the angel.

Figure 2

Figure 3

Uses for the Angel:

1. Use it for a Christmas decoration.

2. Print a Scripture verse on the angel's skirt, and use it as a verse reminder.

© Shining Star Publications

SS20001

© Shining Star Publications

Paper Bags

Pattern

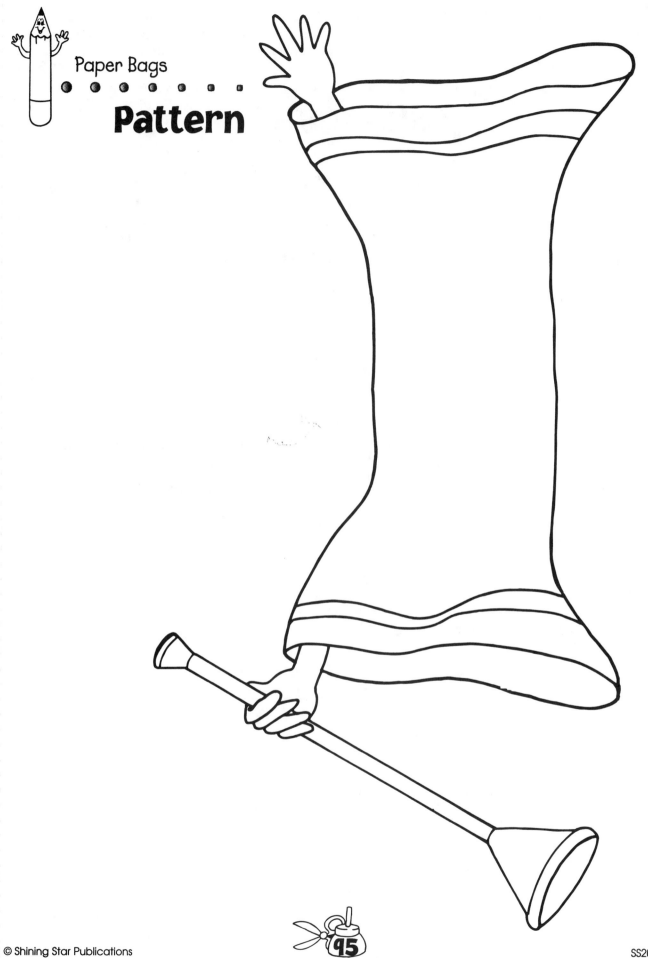

SS20001

Paper Bags

Fish Puppet

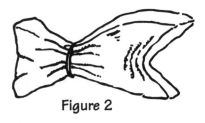

Materials:
lunch bag
eyes and mouth pattern on page 97
crayons
scissors
rubber band
glue

Directions:

1. Color and cut out the eyes and mouth patterns.

Figure 1

2. Open the bag and place your hand inside. The bag should be placed with the flattened end longways as shown in Figure 1.

3. Push the center of the flattened end toward the middle of your hand to form the fish's mouth.

4. Place the rubber band around the bag and your arm, then fluff the bag to make the fish's tail (Figure 2).

5. Glue the eyes and mouth to the fish puppet.

Figure 2

Uses for the Fish Puppet:

1. Use it to retell such Bible stories as "The Miraculous Catch of Fish" (John 21), "Creation" (Genesis 1), "Jonah" (Jonah 1–2), and "The Fish That Helped Pay Taxes" (Matthew 17:24-27).

2. Act out Bible stories using your fish puppet.

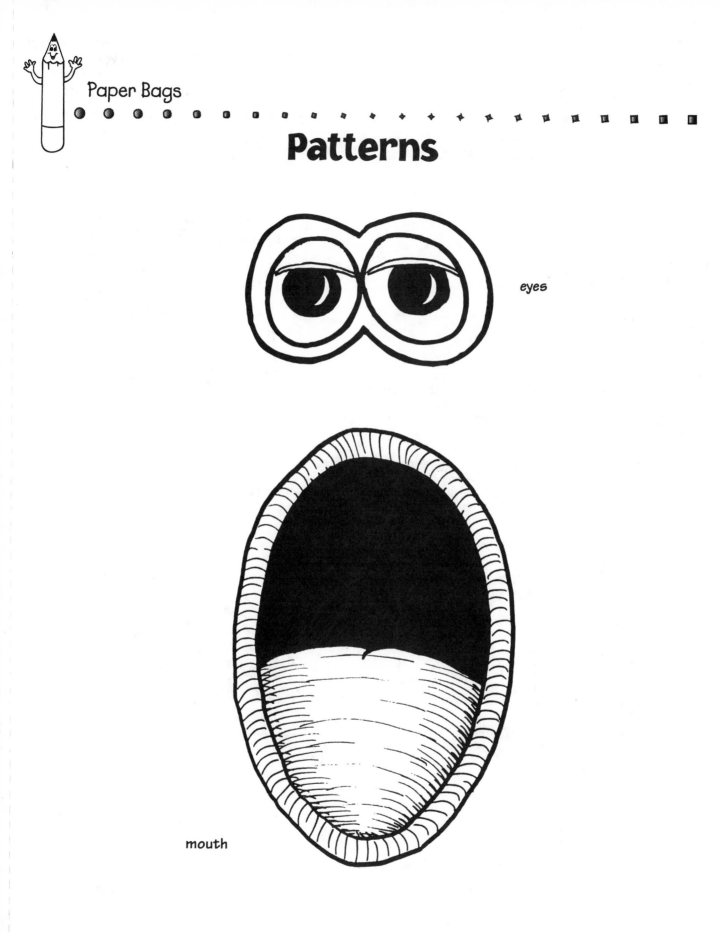

Patterns

eyes

mouth

© Shining Star Publications

SS20001

Paper Bags

Stand-Up Story Bag

Here's a fun way to illustrate Bible stories!

Materials:
lunch bag (larger bag if preferred)
paper for stuffing
preprinted Bible story picture
scissors
double-sided tape
tape

Directions:
1. Fill the bag with paper to make it stand better.

2. Fold over the top of the bag and tape it in place (Figure 1).

3. Cut out the Bible story picture (Figure 2).

4. Place double-sided tape behind the corners of the picture and attach it to the side of the bag.

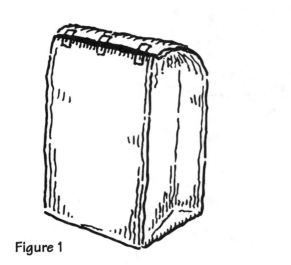

Figure 1

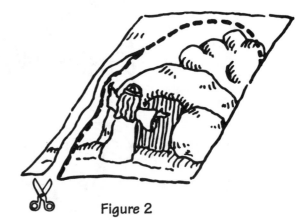

Figure 2

Uses for the Story Bag:
1. Use the story bag when telling a Bible story.

2. Put objects in the bag relating to the story. Use them as props when you retell it.

48

© Shining Star Publications

SS20001

But when she could hide him (Moses) no longer, she got a papyrus basket for him and coated it with tar and pitch. (Exodus 2:3a)

Woven Basket

Materials:

lunch bag
ruler
scissors
three or four 18"–20" paper strips
one 12" strip of paper
glue
pencil

Directions:

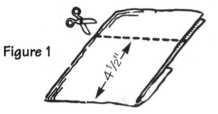

Figure 1

4½"

1. Measure 4½" from the bottom of the flattened bag and mark it for your cutting line.

2. Cut across the folded bag on the cutting line (Figure 1).

3. Open the remaining portion of the bag and set it on a flat surface.

4. Fold in the top of the bag so it touches the bottom of the bag (Figure 2). Note: Fold the bag as smoothly as possible.

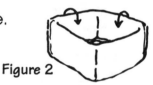

Figure 2

5. Cut slits through the folded parts of the bag, leaving approximately ½" uncut near the bottom (Figure 3). Caution: Do not cut all the way down to the bottom of the bag.

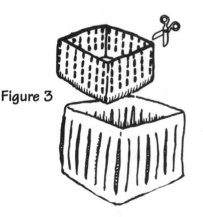

Figure 3

6. Gently pull out the folded part of the bag.

7. Using the paper strips, begin weaving in and out of the slits in the bag. Glue the ends together when you finish (Figure 4).

8. Glue the 12" strip of paper to two sides to form a handle.

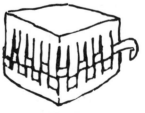

Figure 4

Uses for the Basket:

1. Use it to retell stories that include baskets, such as "Baby Moses in the Basket" (Exodus 2:1–10) and "The Feeding of the 5,000" (Matthew 14:14–21).

2. Discuss Bible-time customs and the process of weaving for making baskets and clothing.

3. Use the basket for a decoration or fill it with flowers, treats, or fruits for a gift.

99

© Shining Star Publications

SS20001

God made the wild animals . . . the livestock . . . and all the creatures that move along the ground according to their kinds. And God saw that it was good. (Genesis 1:25)

"Critter" Bag

Materials:
lunch bag
scissors
patterns on page 101
crayons or markers
glue
yarn, ribbon, or string
cotton ball or pom-pon
pencil
ruler

Directions:
1. Fold the bag in half lengthwise and mark the center.

2. To make ears, cut curved lines from the top corners down to approximately 6" from the bottom of the flattened bag (Figure 1).

3. Open the remaining portion of the bag and set it on a flat surface.

4. Color and cut out the animal face pattern to be glued on the bag.

5. Glue the face in place. Add a pom-pon, cotton ball, or yarn at the back for a tail (Figure 2).

6. Tie the ears together with yarn, ribbon, or string.

Figure 1

Uses for the "Critter" Bag:
1. Use it to retell stories including animals, such as "Noah's Ark," "Christ's Triumphal Entry Into Jerusalem," "Mary and Joseph's Trip to Bethlehem," etc.

2. Use the bag for a decoration or fill it with flowers, treats, or fruits for a gift.

Figure 2

© Shining Star Publications

SS20001

Paper Bags

Patterns

bunny

donkey

© Shining Star Publications

101

SS20001

Create Your Own Stationery

God wants us to be encouragers. Make this stationery and use it to write encouraging notes to others.

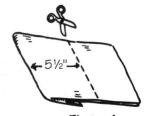

Materials:

white or colored bag (about 6" across), scissors, patterns on page 103, crayons or markers, pencil and pen, ribbon or stickers, ruler

Directions:

1. Prepare note cards this way:

   a. Color and cut out a stationery pattern.

   b. Write an appropriate message on the stationery.

   c. When envelopes (see below) are prepared, place the stationery in the bottom of the "bag" envelope (Figure 3).

   Figure 1

2. Prepare envelopes this way:

   a. Measure 5½" from the bottom edge of a flattened bag and mark it lightly with a pencil.

   b. Cut on the marked line (Figure 1).

   c. Fold the cut edge over and crease the fold so it is even with the bottom of the folded bag (Figure 2).

   d. Open the bag and place your note card in the bottom (Figure 3).

   e. Fold the cut edge over and seal it with a sticker, or wrap a ribbon (about 20") around the envelope and tie it into a bow.

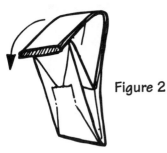

Figure 2

Figure 3

Uses for the Stationery:

1. Prepare note cards with memory verses on them to be taken home and reviewed.

2. Print a note card with a special message to send to a sick classmate or to encourage your pastor, a missionary, a teacher, etc.

3. Make several note cards and envelopes and use them as invitations to a church event or party.

© Shining Star Publications

A note from _____

_____

_____

_____

_____

_____

A note from _____

_____

_____

_____

_____

A note from _____

_____

_____

_____

_____

© Shining Star Publications

SS20001

". . . Even the winds and
the waves obey him!"
(Matthew 8:27)

Message Pinwheel

Materials:

large grocery bag
pencil
permanent marker
unsharpened pencil with eraser
crayons
masking tape
scissors
pushpin

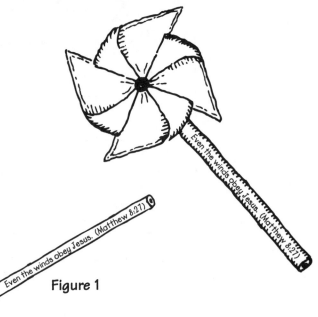

Directions:

1. Using a permanent marker, print on a strip of masking tape the words based on Matthew 8:27: "Even the winds obey Jesus." (Figure 1) Wrap the message tape around the pencil.

Figure 1

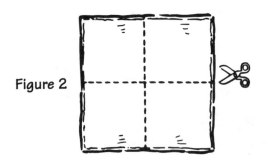

Figure 2

2. Cut the bag apart. Cut a large square from the paper bag, completely removing the side seams and the bottom.

3. Fold the large square in half, then fold again. This will give you four smaller squares. Cut these apart (Figure 2).

4. Color a square with bright colored crayons.

5. Cut slits in the square, beginning at each corner and moving toward the center (Figure 3). (Cutting lines can be marked if necessary.)

6. Fold every other corner into the center and fix it firmly into the pencil eraser by inserting a pushpin.

7. Use the other three squares to make additional pinwheels.

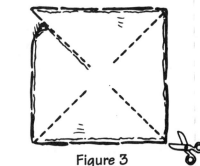

Figure 3

Uses for the Pinwheel:

1. Use it to retell the story of Jesus calming the storm (Matthew 8:23–27).

2. After making the pinwheel, go outside on a windy day to see if it blows in the wind.

3. Write happy messages on the tape which will be wrapped around the pencils. Give the completed pinwheels as gifts to other children.

© Shining Star Publications

SS20001

Paper Bags

Joseph's Robe

Materials:

large, flat shopping bag (usually available at clothing stores)
scissors
crayons or markers
yarn
ruler

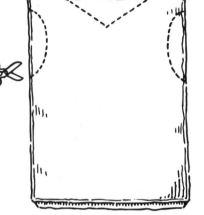

Figure 1

Directions:

1. Cut the bag as shown in Figure 1, making the appropriate 10" armholes and V-neck opening.

2. Color the robe in bright colors.

3. Put the robe on. Wear it unbelted or tie a piece of yarn around the waist for a belt.

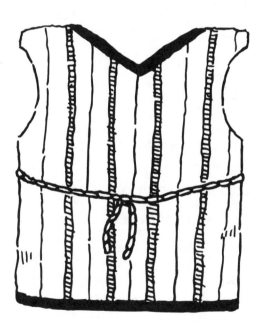

Uses for the Robe:

1. Use the robe to retell the story "Joseph's Coat of Many Colors" in Genesis 37:3–4.

2. Wear your robe in a Bible story drama pantomime.

3. Use the robe to spark a discussion on the different clothing styles of Bible-time people.

© Shining Star Publications

SS20001

"Do not come any closer," God said. "Take off your sandals, for the place where you are standing is holy ground." (Exodus 3:5)

"Simple" Sandals

Materials:
heavy grocery bags, pencil, scissors, ruler, tape

Directions:

1. Trace around your foot (Figure 1).

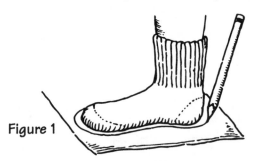

Figure 1

2. Trim ½" outside the marked foot pattern (Figure 2).

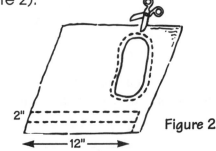

2"

12"

Figure 2

3. Carefully cut a 1" slit between the big toe and the second toe (Figure 3).

4. Measure and cut a 12" x 2" strip from the remainder of the bag (Figure 2). Fold the strip in half.

Figure 3

5. Place one end of the strip in the 1" slit of the sandal and tape it in place on the back side (Figure 4).

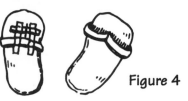

Figure 4

6. Loop the remaining portion of the strip around the front for the big toe and back around the bottom of the sandal, then joining it again through the hole (Figure 4).

7. Adjust the "toe band" so it fits and tape the strip securely in the back.

8. Repeat steps 1–7 for the other sandal.

Uses for the Sandals:

1. Use them to retell any story involving shoes or feet, such as "Moses and the Burning Bush" (Exodus 3:1–10), "Mary Washes Jesus' Feet" (Luke 7:36–48), and "Jesus Washes His Disciples' Feet" (John 13:1–17).

2. Discuss the clothing customs of Bible times.

3. Write a Scripture verse on each sandal and use them as a memory reminder.

© Shining Star Publications

SS20001

Money Bag

People in Bible times usually kept their money in
bags. Make this craft. Then read John 12:3–6 to
find out who was in charge of the disciples'
money bag.

Materials:

plain white paper, coins, crayons, tape, scissors,
lunch bag (or a smaller bag if you prefer), string
or yarn

Directions:

Figure 1

1. Fold a piece of paper in half and
   place several coins sandwiched
   inside—tape if needed (Figure 1).

2. On one side of the paper, do a "crayon
   rub" over the coins (Figure 2).

3. Carefully remove the coins; then cut out
   the paper coins.

4. Puff out the paper bag and place the
   coins in it.

5. Gather the bag together at the top and
   tie a piece of string or yarn around it.

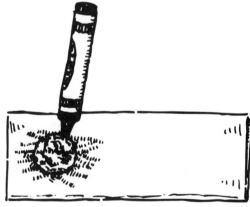

Figure 2

Uses for the Coins and Bag:

1. Use them to retell any story about money (coins) or giving ("Treasures in Heaven"
   Matthew 6:19–24, "Judas Betrays Jesus" Matthew 27:3–4).

2. Discuss the different values of money from various countries or from Bible times.

3. Write words from a Scripture verse on the back of each coin; then remove the coins
   from the bag and place them in proper sequence.

© Shining Star Publications

SS20001

. . . Jacob was a quiet man, staying among the tents. (Genesis 25:27)

Jacob's Tent

Materials:
grocery bag (or smaller)
tape or glue
crayons or markers

Directions:

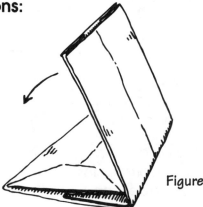

Figure 1

1. Place the bag in a flattened position. Fold the top half over the bottom half as shown in Figure 1.

2. Fold the remaining 3" of the top of the bag even with the other folded edge (Figure 2).

3. Open the bag and place the bottom on a flat surface.

Figure 2

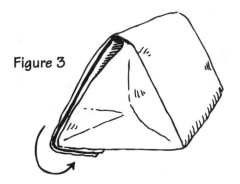

Figure 3

4. Starting at the top, fold the bag on the middle and top crease.

5. The top crease should fit snugly under the "tent" bottom. Tape or glue this into place (Figure 3).

6. Gently color the tent using crayons or markers.

Uses for the Tent:

1. Use the tent to tell about shelters Bible people had.

2. Use the tent to visualize a discussion on Bible customs and home life.

3. Add Bible people and animal figures next to the tent to make a Bible story scene.

© Shining Star Publications

SS20001

Paper Bags

Cornucopia

Make this craft to remind yourself of all the things God gives us. Fill the cornucopia with some of the things He provides.

Materials:
grocery bag; pencil; scissors; glue or tape; stickers, rubber stamps, and/or crayons; construction paper strips (use scraps if available); treats: grapes, raisins, nuts, small candies, etc.; plate

Directions:
1. Place a flattened bag on your work surface and trace a 10" circle on it. A plate can serve as a guide (Figure 1).

2. Cut out the circle.

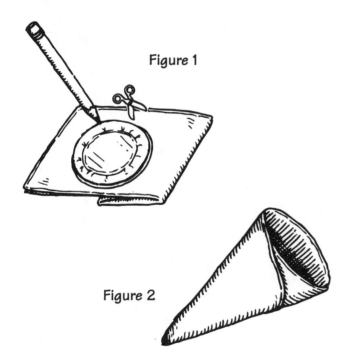

Figure 1

Figure 2

3. Fold the circle in half. On the fold, draw a line from the center of the circle to the edge. Cut along this line.

4. Decorate the half circle with stickers, rubber stamps, and/or crayons.

5. Overlap the cut edges of the half circle and glue together to form a cone (Figure 2).

6. To form a handle, cut a strip of construction paper and attach it to the cone.

7. When dry, fill the cornucopia with tasty treats.

Uses for the Cornucopia:
1. Make a cornucopia for a table decoration to use at a Thanksgiving party.

2. Fill it with treats and give it as a gift or award to someone.

3. Print Scripture verses about Thanksgiving on one side and use it as a memory reminder.

© Shining Star Publications

SS20001

Bible Verse Piñata

Learning Bible verses can be fun! This craft will show you how.

Materials:

large grocery bag
Bible verses or phrases typed or
   printed on small strips of paper
tape
small treats and/or party favors
string or cording
colored tissue paper
glue
blindfold
long stick or broom handle
scissors

Directions:

1. Securely tape Scripture strips to the treats and party favors.

2. Place the treats and favors inside the bag. Twist the top closed and tie tightly with string or cording.

3. Cut 2" circles from tissue paper. Twist them in the center to form flower shapes. Dip the center of each flower in glue and attach it to the outside of the bag. You may also glue strips of tissue paper to the bottom of the bag for decoration.

4. Give the piñata time to dry, then attach it to a tree limb (outside) or hang it from your classroom ceiling.

5. Take turns taking three strikes with the stick at the hanging piñata. Take turns swinging the stick at the piñata until the bag breaks and the treats spill out!

Uses for the Bible Verse Piñata:

1. Children in Mexico often celebrate holidays and special occasions by breaking open a piñata. Research Mexico.

2. Write several sets of individual words for a Scripture verse and attach the word strips to the treats. After you pick up the treats, gather into groups and put the words into proper order.

3. Make smaller variations of the piñata to display as decorations.

110

© Shining Star Publications

Craft Stick Figures

Materials:
French fry bags (given free at some fast-food restaurants); patterns on pages 112–114; crayons; glue or glue sticks; craft sticks; yarn, string, ribbon, or cotton balls (optional)

Directions:
1. Use a French fry bag for each figure you want to make.

2. Choose and color a face pattern, cut it out, and glue it to the bag (Figure 1).

3. Glue the craft stick to the inside of the bag.

4. Color and cut out the arms and legs patterns and glue them to the French fry bag "body."

5. Yarn, string, curling ribbon, or cotton balls may be added for hair, beards, animal tails, etc.

6. Other accessory patterns are included on page 114. Each may be colored, cut out, and glued to the appropriate figure.

Figure 1

Uses for the Craft Stick Figures:
1. Use these figures to act out a Bible story.

2. Make characters such as Daniel, David, and Zacchaeus to use when singing songs about them.

3. Use the figures as puppets to tell a story.

4. Print a Bible verse about the Bible person or animal on the back of it and use it as a Scripture reminder.

© Shining Star Publications

SS20001

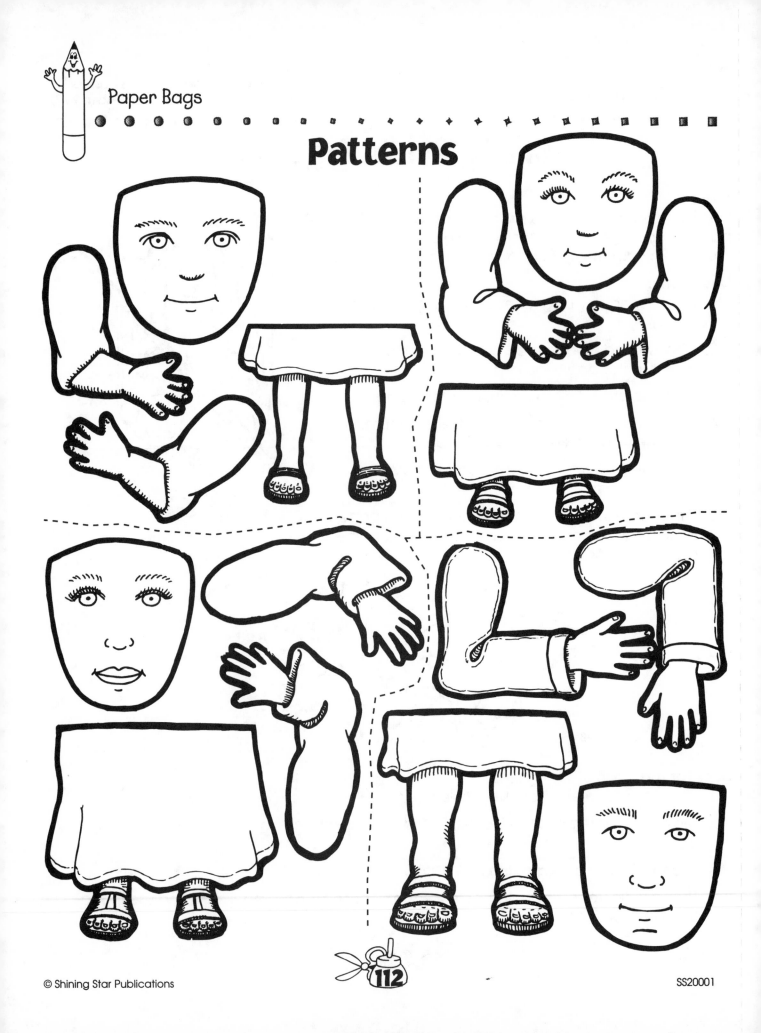

Patterns

© Shining Star Publications

112

Patterns

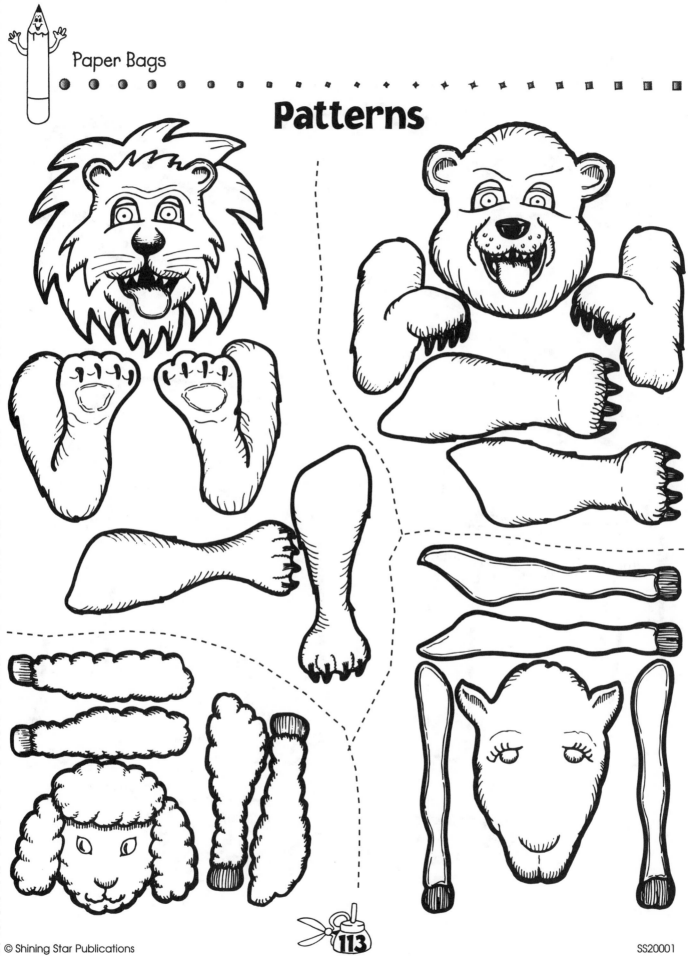

© Shining Star Publications

SS20001

Patterns

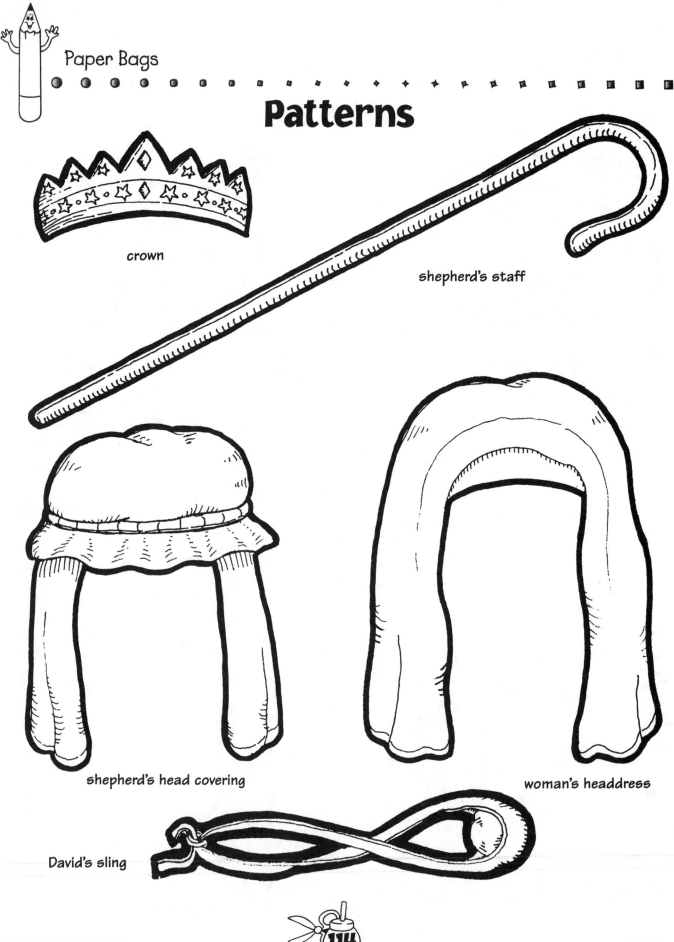

crown

shepherd's staff

shepherd's head covering

woman's headdress

David's sling

114

© Shining Star Publications

SS20001

Paper Bags

Classy Mural

Materials:
large grocery bag; scissors; crayons, markers, or tempera paint, paintbrushes, small jars, rags, and paint shirts (if using paint); wide masking tape

Directions:

1. Cut the bag apart, starting at the side seam and cutting to the bottom. Remove the bottom of the bag completely.

2. Open the bag and lay it flat on your work surface.

3. Using crayons, markers, or paints, illustrate a Bible story or theme on the paper bag.

4. Let the painted picture dry completely.

5. Attach your picture and those of your classmates together in a quiltlike fashion using wide masking tape. Join one picture to the next by taping the backs together (Figure 1).

6. When all the pictures have been connected, display the large picture on a wall or bulletin board. You now have a "classy" mural!

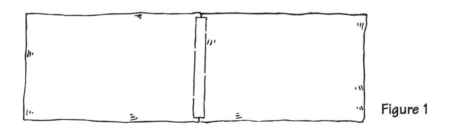

Figure 1

Ideas for the Mural:

1. Use it to retell a Bible story.

2. Draw pictures of important holidays (Easter, July 4th, Thanksgiving, Christmas, etc.) and display them in this manner.

3. Make a mural of your church's history.

4. Draw pictures to illustrate days of Creation or a Bible time line.

© Shining Star Publications

SS20001

Paper Bags

*And God said, " . . . let birds
fly above the earth across
the expanse of the sky."*
(Genesis 1:20)

Little Quacker

Materials:

French fry bag, tape, glue, yellow or light orange
felt, pencil, beads or wiggle eyes, scissors,
patterns below

Directions:

1. Wrap a French fry bag lengthwise into a
   circular shape and tape or glue the ends
   together (Figure 1).

2. Pinch the top of the circular bag together
   and glue or tape it closed (Figure 2).

3. Trace the patterns on felt and cut them out.

4. Tape or glue the wings and the bill to the bag.

5. Glue on beads or wiggle eyes for the eyes.

6. To work the puppets, place your fingers inside the bag.

Figure 1

Figure 2

Uses for the Little Quacker:

1. Use it to tell the story of Noah's Ark from a duck's perspective.

2. Use it to tell others how God loves and cares for all His creatures.

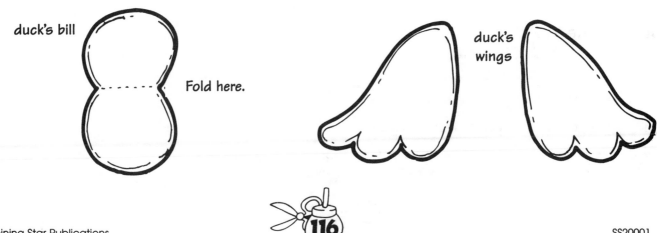

duck's bill

Fold here.

duck's
wings

© Shining Star Publications

SS20001

Paper Bags

Paper Flowers

Materials:

French fry bags (one per flower)
pipe cleaners
artificial leaves or pattern below
green crayons or markers
glue
scissors

Directions:

1. Place one hand inside a French fry bag. With the other hand, push the bottom center of the bag upward around your fingers inside the bag (Figure 1).

2. While holding the inside fold with your fingers, pinch the outside corners together and twist several times to form a stem (Figure 2).

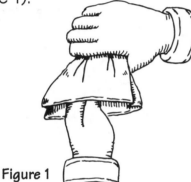

Figure 1

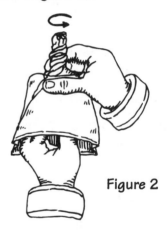

Figure 2

3. Color and cut out the leaf pattern or use an artificial leaf.

4. Glue the leaf next to the short stem of the flower.

5. To make a long stem, wrap a pipe cleaner around the flower stem.

6. Make several flowers, experimenting with the twisting of the paper to make rosebuds or more open flowers.

Uses for the Paper Flowers:

1. Use them as pretty party decorations or thoughtful Mother's Day gifts.

2. Use them to decorate a bulletin board depicting God's beautiful creation.

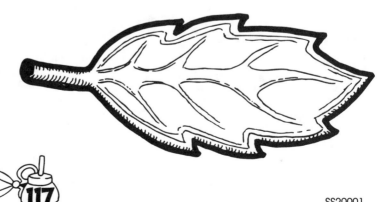

© Shining Star Publications

117

SS20001

In the Beginning Bookmark

Materials:

white posterboard, scissors, colored tissue paper, water, paintbrush, markers, hole punch, yarn, tape, ruler

Directions:

1. Cut the posterboard into 2½" x 6" strips (bookmarks).

2. Tear small pieces of tissue paper about 1" x 1½" in size, using colors appropriate for the part of Creation you wish to represent (mountains, woods, oceans, sky, etc.).

3. Brush water over the bookmark. Add colored tissue paper pieces and let dry.

4. Pull off the tissue paper and use a marker to write "God made the _____." (add the part of Creation you are presenting) on the bookmark.

5. Punch holes about ½" apart around the edges of the bookmark.

6. Cut a 36" piece of yarn. Lace the yarn through the holes in the sides of the bookmark. Make sure you tape the ends down.

Other Ideas:

1. Make bookmarks to illustrate other Bible passages.

2. Omit tissue paper and draw a picture of Creation on the bookmark.

3. Omit lacing.

4. Before punching holes and lacing edges, cover the bookmark with clear adhesive plastic for more permanency.

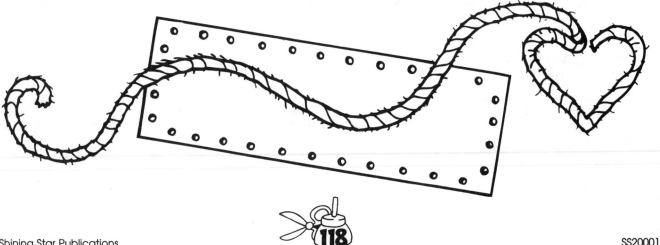

© Shining Star Publications

SS20001

Then God said, "Let the land produce vegetation . . ."
(Genesis 1:11)

See What God Made Collage

Materials:
cardboard, blue tempera paint, paintbrush, nature objects, glue, scissors

Directions:
1. Cut a square of cardboard to the desired size.

2. Paint the square.

3. Go on a nature walk and gather small items suitable for gluing to the cardboard.

4. Glue the objects you found to the cardboard square.

5. Hang the collage to remind you to celebrate the many wonderful things God has put into our world.

Other Ideas:
1. Add this phrase to the bottom of the picture: "Thank God for His Wonderful World."

2. Glue nature objects to colored posterboard.

3. Cover cardboard with burlap before adding objects.

Thank God for His Wonderful World.

© Shining Star Publications

SS20001

*"I am going to bring
floodwaters on the earth . . ."*
(Genesis 6:17)

Safe From the Flood

Materials:

posterboard, scissors, pencil, fine-line markers,
stapler, patterns on pages 121 and 122

Directions:

Ark

1. Cut out the ark pattern.

2. Trace around and cut out the ark pattern
   from posterboard. Cut out the ark door.

3. Fold the ark as indicated below. Fold down
   the door.

4. Staple the ark hull together at the sides.

Noah and Animals

1. Color the animal and people patterns
   using markers.

2. Cut out the figures as indicated on
   page 122. Then fold them so they will stand.

3. Use them with the ark to tell the story of "Noah and the Flood."

Other Ideas:

1. Make the ark from cardboard.

2. Paint the ark, people, and animals.

3. Cover the ark with construction paper.

4. Draw your own pairs of animals to put in the ark.

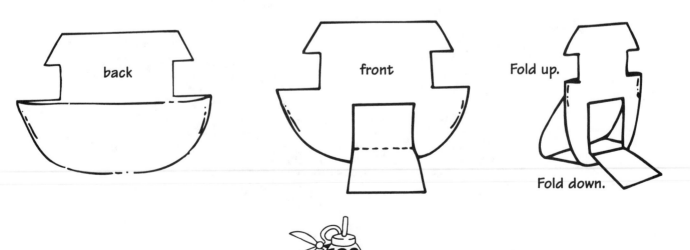

back

front

Fold up.

Fold down.

© Shining Star Publications

SS20001

Pattern

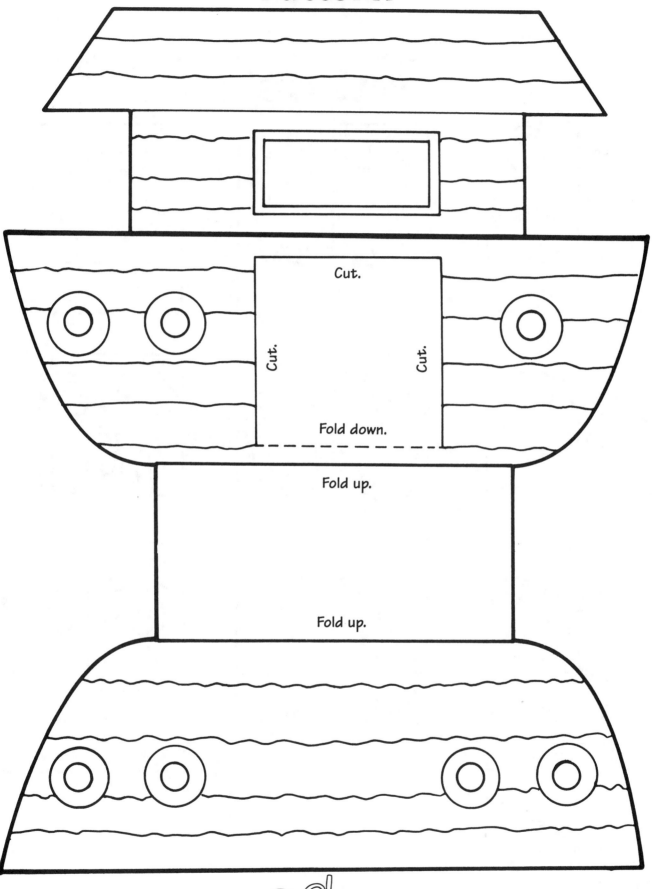

Cut.

Cut.

Cut.

Fold down.

Fold up.

Fold up.

© Shining Star Publications

121

SS20001

Patterns

Cut.

Cut out and fold up.

122

© Shining Star Publications

SS20001

"I have set my rainbow in the clouds . . ."
(Genesis 9:13)

A Rainbow of Promise

God Keeps His Promises

Materials:

blue posterboard (9½" x 11"), fabric scraps in rainbow colors, cotton, glue, scissors, pattern on page 124

Directions:

1. Cut out the pattern.

2. Glue it to posterboard.

3. Cut out square fabric pieces.

4. Glue the fabric squares on the pattern to make a rainbow.

5. Glue cotton to represent a cloud at the bottom of the rainbow.

6. Use a marker to write "God Keeps His Promises" on the poster.

7. Let your rainbow be a reminder that we can rely on God to keep His promises to His people.

Other Ideas:

1. Paint the piece of posterboard blue.

2. Use squares of construction paper instead of fabric to color the rainbow.

3. Color the rainbow with markers.

4. Use a prism to show how light breaks into different colors. Follow the order of prism colors to color the rainbow.

5. Use an overhead projector to enlarge the rainbow pattern on a larger piece of posterboard.

© Shining Star Publications

SS20001

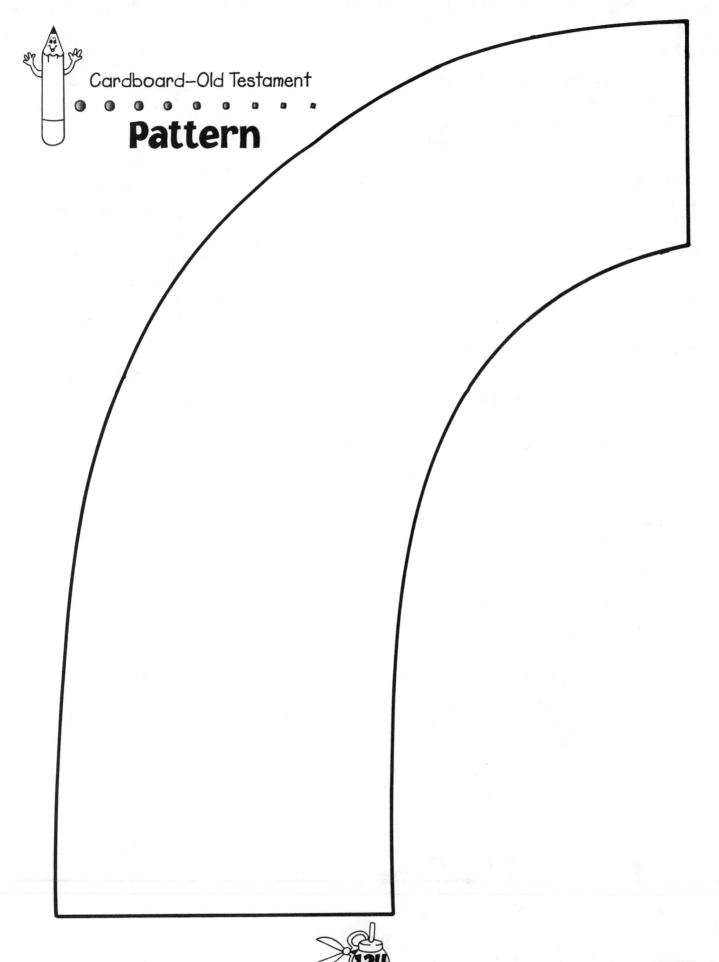

© Shining Star Publications

SS20001

Daniel and the Lions Puppets

Materials:

cardboard, construction paper (yellow and pink), two craft sticks, glue, corrugated cardboard, markers, scissors

Directions:

1. Cut two construction paper circles (one of each color) and two cardboard circles the same size.

2. Glue the construction paper circles to the cardboard circles.

3. Use markers to draw a lion's face on the yellow circle and Daniel's face on the pink circle.

4. Cut strips of corrugated cardboard.

5. Glue the strips in a circle around the lion's face for a mane. Then glue the strips onto Daniel's face for hair and a beard.

6. Tape each circle to a craft stick to make a puppet. Use the puppets to tell the story of how God protected Daniel in the den of hungry lions.

Other Ideas:

1. Glue corrugated cardboard strips around paper plates for masks.

2. Draw faces on circles cut from posterboard.

© Shining Star Publications

125

SS20001

The Lord Is My Shepherd

Materials:
white posterboard
scissors
glue
cotton
craft stick
Styrofoam™ cup
fine-line markers
patterns on page 127

Directions:

1. Cut out the patterns.

2. Trace around and cut out a posterboard sheep.

3. Use markers to outline the sheep's eye and mouth and to color the caption "The Lord Is My Shepherd."

4. Glue the craft stick and cotton to the sheep.

5. Trim the Styrofoam™ cup 2" from the bottom. Set it upside down and glue the caption on it.

6. Stick the bottom of the craft stick into the cup.

7. Let your sheep be a reminder that your loving Lord cares for you like a shepherd cares for his sheep.

Other Ideas:

1. Omit the cup and use the sheep alone for a puppet.

2. Make a cutout of Jesus, the Good Shepherd, to place beside the sheep.

© Shining Star Publications

126

SS20001

Patterns

The Lord Is
My Shepherd

© Shining Star Publications

SS20001

Our Refuge and Strength

Materials:

cardboard, glue, scissors, pencil, construction paper,
felt-tip markers, heavy-duty stapler, patterns on
page 129

Directions:

1. Cut out the patterns.

2. Cut an 18" x 11" rectangular piece of cardboard.

3. Use the rectangular pattern to trace and cut out
   rectangular openings across the top of the
   cardboard (Figure 1).

4. Trace and cut out arched windows from
   construction paper using the window pattern.
   Glue the windows to the sides of the cardboard
   (Figure 1).

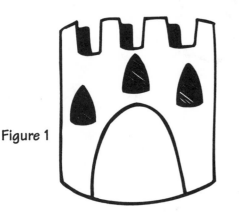

Figure 1

5. Cut out the doorway pattern and use markers to
   decorate it. Glue it at the bottom of the cardboard.

6. Curve the cardboard into a circle. Staple it together
   with a 1" overlap.

7. Let this "castle" serve as a reminder that your strong
   God is always there to help and protect you.

Other Ideas:

1. Omit the pattern pieces and cut
   your own windows and door for the
   castle. Cut an arch for the door and
   write the Bible words on it.

2. Read the rest of Psalm 46, looking
   for other word pictures that tell of
   God's mighty power and protection
   in times of trouble.

© Shining Star Publications

SS20001

Patterns

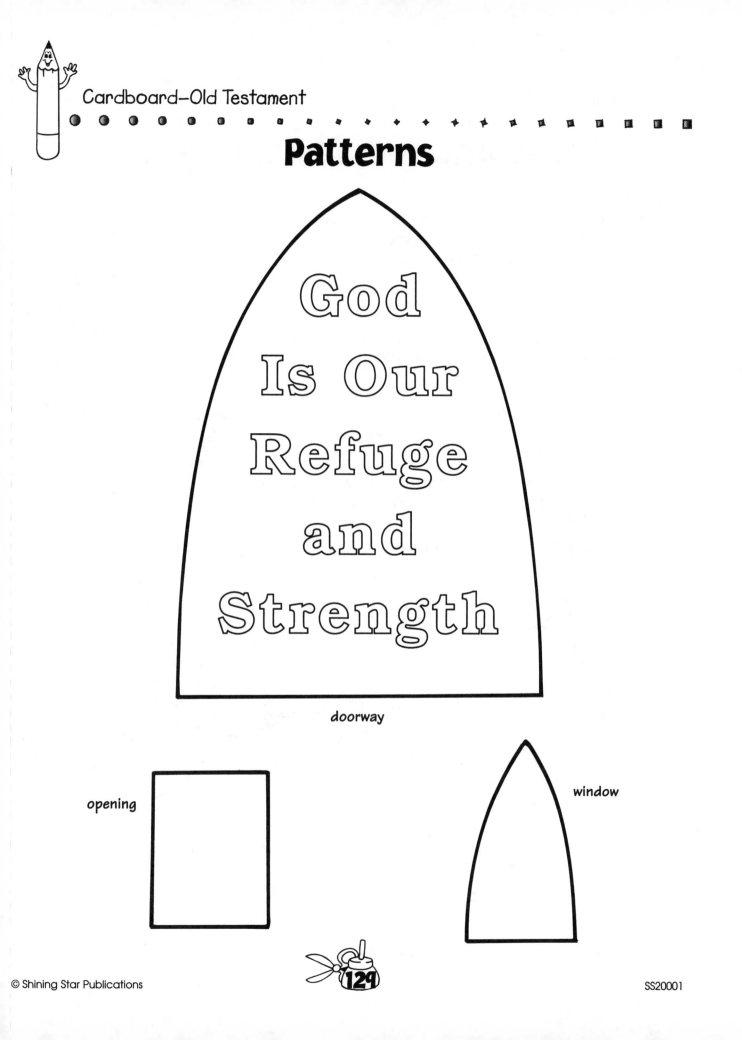

God
Is Our
Refuge
and
Strength

doorway

opening

window

© Shining Star Publications

SS20001

". . . He is to be called John."
(Luke 1:60)

Get Ready for Jesus Wreath

Materials:
corrugated cardboard, scissors, green tempera paint, paintbrush, red tissue paper, markers or crayons, pencil, yarn, hole punch, glue, patterns on page 131

Directions:

1. Cut out the patterns.

2. Trace around and cut out the wreath pattern from corrugated cardboard. Paint it green and let dry.

3. Color and cut out the bow pattern.

4. Glue the bow to the wreath.

5. Punch a hole at the top of the wreath and tie a piece of yarn to it for hanging.

6. Cut twenty-five 1½" x 1½" squares of red tissue paper. Each day of December, wad up a square of tissue paper and glue it to the cardboard wreath.

7. Let the wreath be a daily reminder that Christmas is a time to get ready for Jesus.

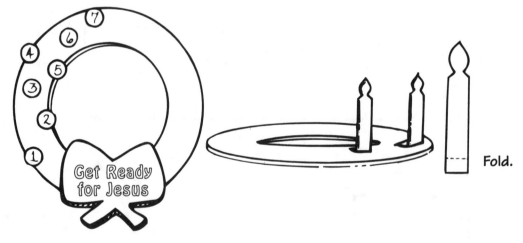

Other Ideas:

1. Paint a flat piece of cardboard and stick round, red stickers to it for each day of Advent.

2. Place a flat, paper wreath with stand-up paper candles glued on it as a centerpiece during Advent.

© Shining Star Publications

SS20001

Patterns

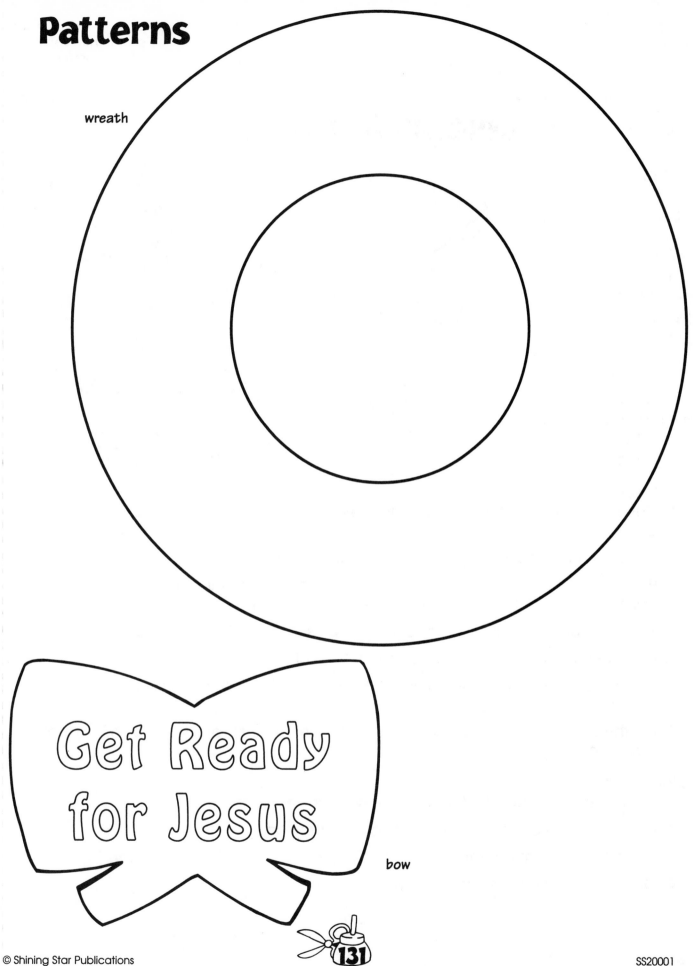

wreath

Get Ready
for Jesus

bow

© Shining Star Publications

131

SS20001

Celebrate His Birth

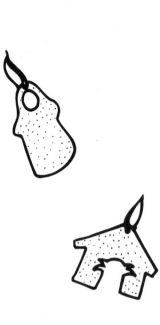

Materials:
cardboard
pencil
glue
pointed scissors
tempera paint
paintbrush
glitter
plastic straws
red plastic tape
Styrofoam™ cup
plastic-based clay
evergreen sprig
ribbon bow
patterns on page 133

Directions:
1. Cut out the patterns that you want to use for your Christmas arrangement.

2. Trace around the patterns on cardboard and cut them out.

3. Paint one side of each cardboard pattern with tempera paint. Sprinkle on glitter while paint is wet. Let dry; then paint the other side.

4. Put stripes on the Styrofoam™ cup with red plastic tape. Glue on the bow.

5. Glue (or tape) a straw to the back of each cardboard figure.

6. Place a ball of plastic-based clay in the bottom of the cup and stick the straw in it. Add the evergreen sprig.

7. Put the arrangement in your home as a reminder to celebrate Jesus' birth, the real reason for the Christmas season.

Other Ideas:
1. Outline and cut out shapes from Christmas cookie cutters.

2. Cut shapes out of Christmas cards and glue them on.

3. Make cup centerpieces to represent different parts of the Christmas story.

4. Omit straw. Hang the symbol with yarn for a tree ornament.

© Shining Star Publications

SS20001

Patterns

angel

Joseph

manger

crown for
wise man

camel

Mary

shepherd

stable

© Shining Star Publications

SS20001

. . . "Do not be afraid. I bring
you good news of great joy that
will be for all the people."
(Luke 1:10)

Christ the Savior Is Born

Materials:
cardboard, glue, markers or crayons, scissors, clear plastic adhesive (optional), patterns on pages 135–139

Directions:

Stable
1. Color and cut out the stable patterns on pages 135 and 136.
2. Glue the patterns on cardboard and cut them out.
3. Cut along the dotted lines on the stable. Insert pieces into the slits on the stable as indicated in diagram on page 136. Fold the tabs and glue in place.
4. Fold and stand up the stable. Add Christmas figures to it (see below).

Figures
1. Color and cut out the patterns you wish to use from pages 137–139. Glue them to cardboard and cut them out.
2. Slightly fold the cardboard figures down the center and stand them up.
3. Let your nativity scene be a reminder of the events that took place when Christ our Savior was born.

© Shining Star Publications

SS20001

Pattern

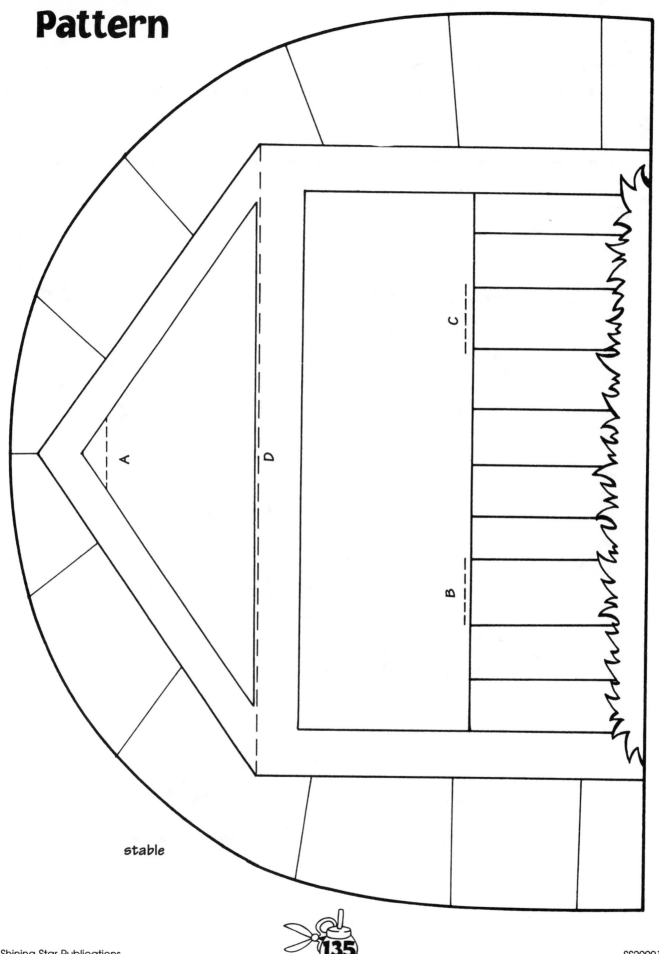

A

B

C

D

stable

© Shining Star Publications

135

Patterns

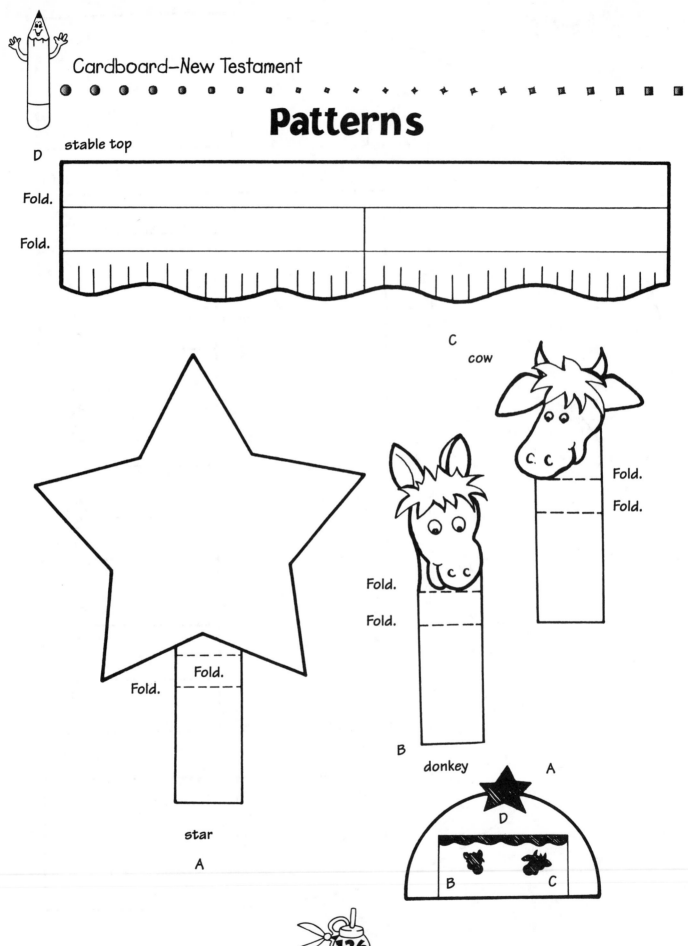

D   stable top

Fold.

Fold.

C   cow

star

A

Fold.

Fold.

B   donkey

A

Fold.

Fold.

Fold.

Fold.

Fold.

D

B   C

© Shining Star Publications   SS20001

Patterns

Joseph

Mary and Jesus

© Shining Star Publications

137

Patterns

shepherd

angel

© Shining Star Publications

SS20001

Patterns

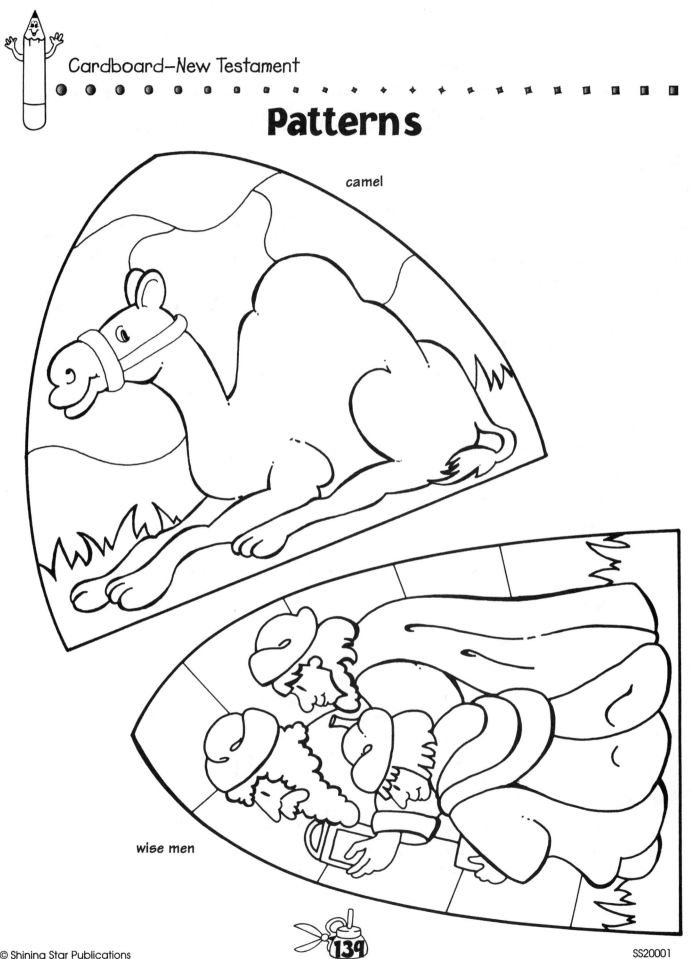

camel

wise men

© Shining Star Publications

SS20001

. . . the Holy Spirit descended
on him . . . like a dove . . .
(Luke 3:22)

A Dove Came Down Mobile

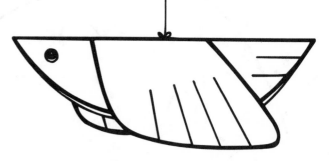

Materials:

white tagboard or posterboard, pencil, scissors, marker, yarn, glue, hole punch, stapler, white feathers (optional), patterns on pages 141–142

Directions: (Adult help may be needed.)

1. Cut out the dove patterns.

2. Trace around the dove patterns on white posterboard and cut them out. Cut slits in wings and body of dove.

3. Use a marker to draw an eye on each side of the dove.

4. Fold the dove's body and staple it together as indicated below.

5. Glue the wings along the top fold of the dove's body.

6. Punch a small hole at the top of the dove and tie a piece of yarn through it for hanging.

7. Glue some white feathers on the dove (optional).

8. Talk about how the Holy Spirit appeared as a dove when Jesus was baptized.

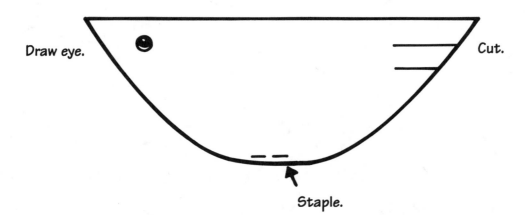

Draw eye.

Cut.

Staple.

Other Ideas:

1. Use it to tell the story of the dove sent out by Noah after the flood.

2. Adapt the bird shape to use with the story of Creation, Elijah and the ravens, or God's care for the flowers as mentioned in the Sermon on the Mount.

© Shining Star Publications

SS20001

Pattern

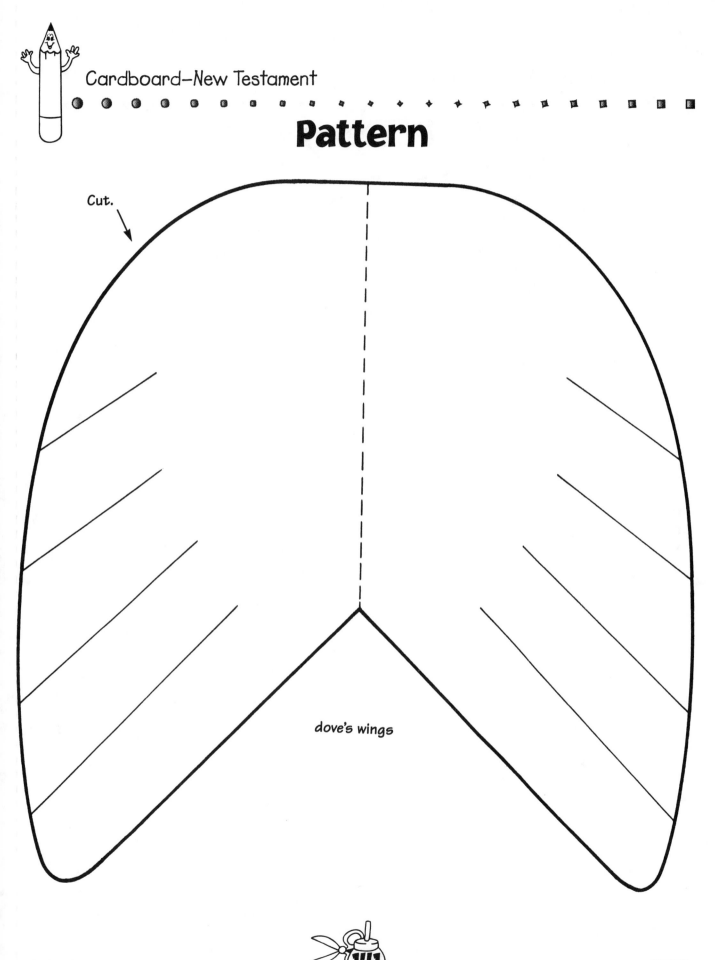

Cut.

dove's wings

© Shining Star Publications

SS20001

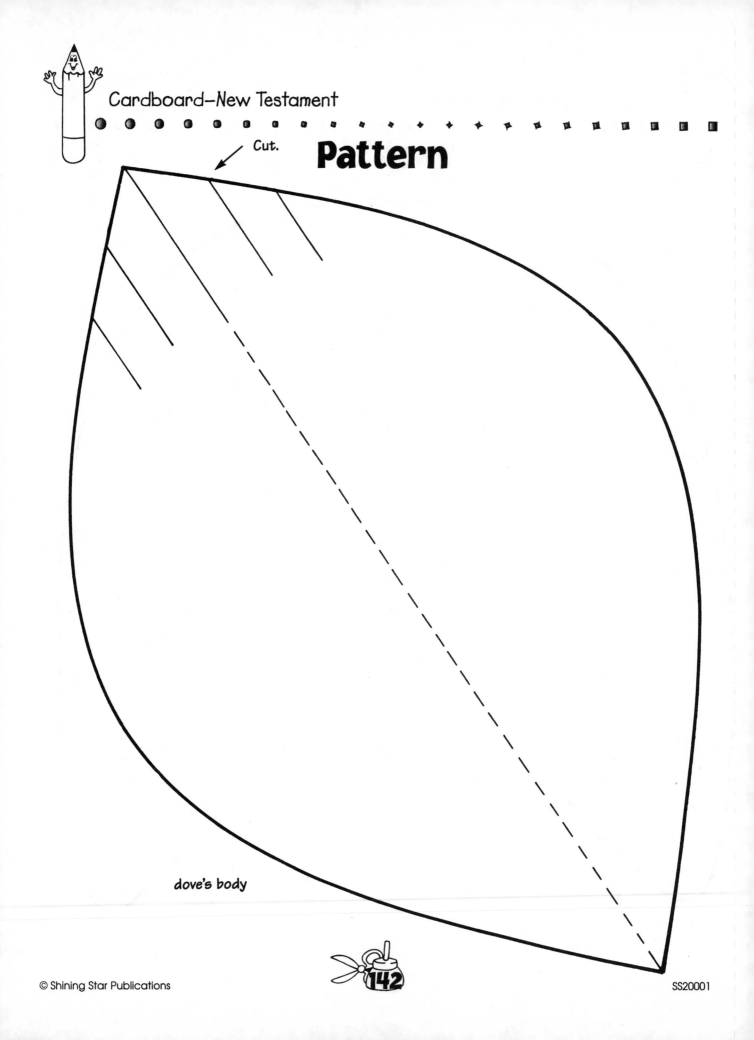

Cut.

Pattern

dove's body

© Shining Star Publications

142

SS20001

"I tell you, get up, take your mat and go home."
(Mark 2:11)

Through the Roof

Materials:
corrugated cardboard
scissors
pencil
fine-line markers
cardboard square (9" x 9")
green and brown construction paper
glue
masking tape
patterns on page 144

Directions: (Adult help may be needed.)

1. Trace around and cut out the house pattern from corrugated cardboard. Cut out the door and the opening flap on top. Fold the flap so it opens and closes.

2. Tear small pieces of construction paper for ground and grass. Glue them over the 9" x 9" cardboard square.

3. Glue the house to the 9" x 9" cardboard square. (Reinforce the sides of the house with masking tape.)

4. Use markers to color the figure patterns and cut them out.

5. Fold the figures so they stand up.

6. Use the house and stand-up figures to act out the story of Jesus healing the paralyzed man (Mark 2:1–12).

Other Ideas:

1. Use an overhead projector to enlarge the patterns. Make figures from clothespins to go with the larger house.

2. Draw your own stand-up figures for Jesus, the paralyzed man, his friends, and others at the house.

3. Paint the cardboard base with tempera paint.

4. Cut the house pattern from plain cardboard.

© Shining Star Publications

SS20001

Patterns

© Shining Star Publications

144

SS20001

. . . "Let the little children come to me . . ."
(Matthew 19:14)

Jesus Loves Me Mobile

Materials:
cardboard
red and white construction paper
white paper doilies
scissors
pencil
masking tape
yarn
marker
glue
overhead projector
pattern on page 146

Directions:

1. Place the pattern on a fold of paper. Trace around it and cut it out to make a full-sized heart. Use the full-sized pattern to cut out a cardboard heart.

2. Tape a piece of white paper to a wall. Stand between the overhead projector and the paper so that your shadow falls on the paper. Have a friend or an adult outline your silhouette and cut it out.

3. Cover both sides of the heart with red construction paper.

4. Glue pieces of paper doilies on the heart (leave room for the message).

5. Write the words "Jesus Loves (your name)" on the heart.

6. Have an adult use sharp scissors to punch one hole at the top of the silhouette and another at the top of the heart, one hole a couple of inches below the other.

7. Use a piece of yarn to tie the silhouette to the bottom hole. Use a second piece of yarn to tie the heart so it hangs like a mobile. Let your silhouette mobile remind you that Jesus loves you.

Other Ideas:

1. Use black, tan, or pink paper for the silhouette.

2. Add stickers, pieces of bright ribbon, or other decorative scraps to the heart.

3. Use yarn and/or markers to add hair and other features to the silhouette.

4. Paint the heart and silhouette with tempera paint.

© Shining Star Publications

145

SS20001

Pattern

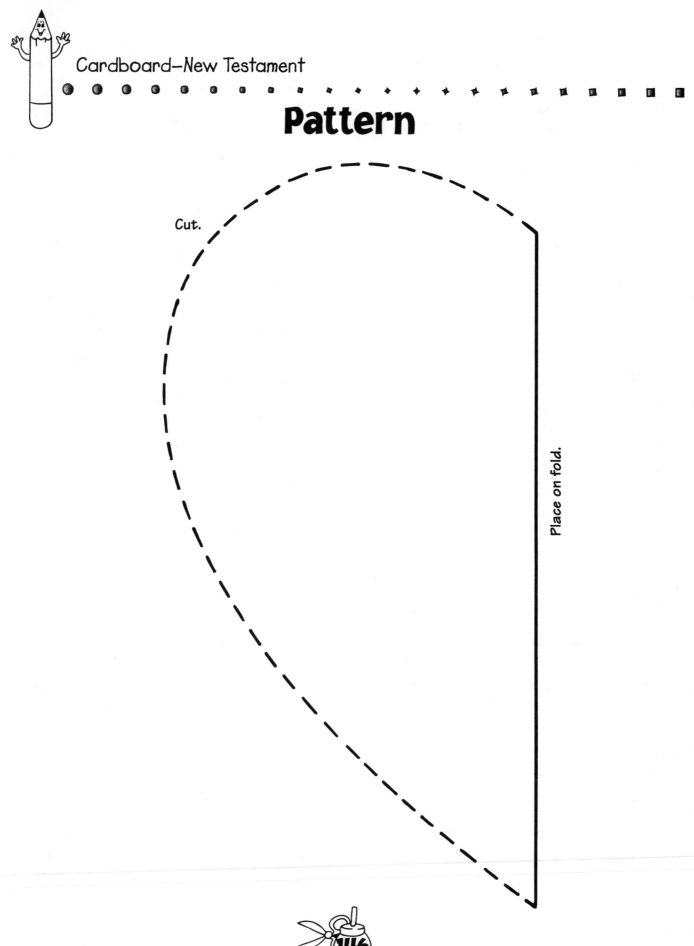

Cut.

Place on fold.

© Shining Star Publications

146

SS20001

Jesus said to them, "I did one miracle, and you are all astonished."
(John 7:21)

Jesus Helps People Puppets

Materials:
cardboard
glue
scissors
markers or crayons
craft sticks
two cardboard tubes
clear plastic adhesive (optional)
patterns on pages 148–150

Bibleland Theater

Directions:

Tabletop Puppet Theater
1. Cut out the theater pattern. Glue the theater to cardboard and cut it out.
2. Use markers to decorate the theater. For more permanency, cover with clear plastic adhesive.
3. Glue an upright cardboard tube to each side of the theater on the back to make it stand up.
4. Stand the theater at the edge of a table. Use puppets behind it to tell stories of Jesus and His love for other people.

Puppets
1. Choose puppet patterns on pages 149–150 to illustrate the Bible story you wish to retell. Cut out the patterns.
2. Glue the patterns to cardboard and cut them out.
3. Use markers to decorate each puppet. Cover them with clear plastic adhesive for more permanency.
4. Glue craft sticks to the back of the puppets for handles.

Other Ideas:
1. Use tempera to paint the puppets and theater.
2. Make a variety of puppets for use with Bible stories throughout the year.
3. Write scripts for puppet presentations.

© Shining Star Publications

SS20001

Bibleland Theater

148

© Shining Star Publications

SS20001

Patterns

Jesus

© Shining Star Publications

Patterns

© Shining Star Publications

SS20001

. . . "Blessed is he who comes
in the name of the Lord!"
(Mark 11:9)

Sing Hosanna

Materials:
corrugated cardboard
pencil
scissors
green tempera paint
paintbrush
markers or crayons
glue
patterns on page 152

Directions: (Adult help may be needed.)

1. Trace around the palm pattern on corrugated cardboard with lines going in a horizontal direction to the sides of the branch as illustrated above. Cut it out.

2. Paint one side of the cardboard branch green.

3. Fringe sides of the branch by cutting triangular slits along the cardboard ridges (optional).

4. Cut out and color the "Sing Hosanna" pattern. Glue it to the center of the palm branch.

5. Put up your completed palm branch as a reminder of Jesus' triumphant entry into Jerusalem when people waved palm branches and sang "Hosanna" to Jesus, their King.

Other Ideas:

1. Do your own lettering for the "Sing Hosanna" strip.

2. Write the words to a Palm Sunday song in the center of the palm branch.

3. Cut the branch out of plain cardboard; then color it with crayons or paint it.

4. Use the branches for a Palm Sunday procession.

5. Mount the branches on a Palm Sunday bulletin board.

© Shining Star Publications

SS20001

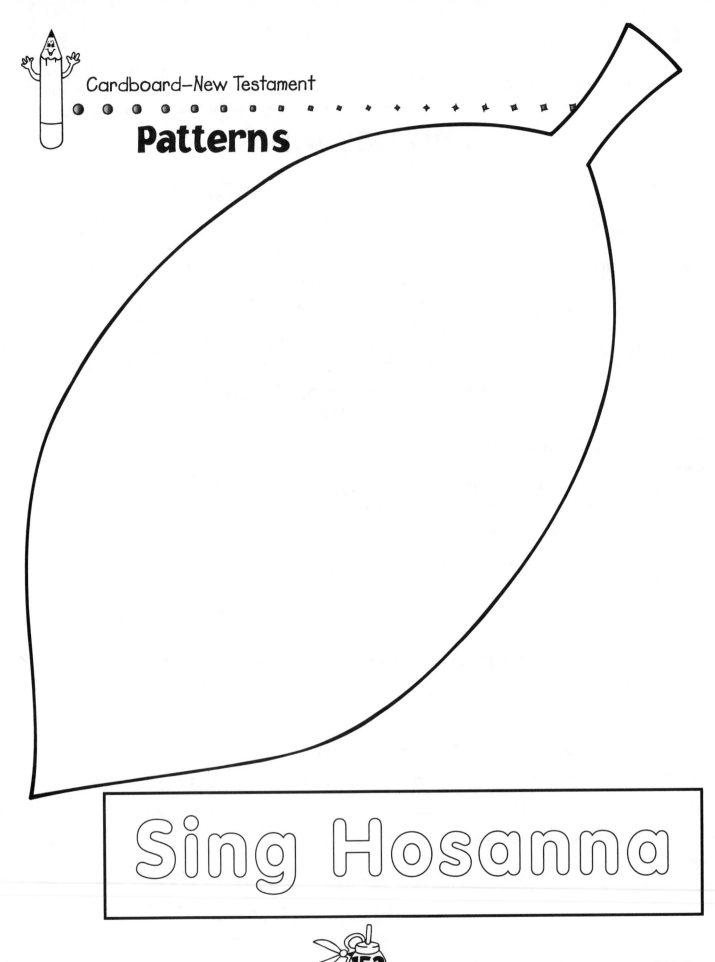

Sing Hosanna

© Shining Star Publications

SS20001

He Is Risen

Materials:

9½" x 11" piece of cardboard, blue tempera paint, paintbrush, corrugated cardboard, burlap, leaves, newspaper, heavy book, glue, masking tape, markers, paper clip, scissors, pencil, patterns on page 154

Directions: (Adult help may be needed.)

1. Press leaves by placing them between several layers of newspaper and setting them under a heavy book for several days.

2. Cut out the patterns.

3. Cut a piece of burlap large enough to cover the bottom three-fourths of the 9½" x 11" piece of cardboard. Glue on the burlap.

4. To represent the sky, paint the cardboard blue in the area above the burlap. Let dry.

5. Trace and cut out the tomb and stone patterns from corrugated cardboard.

6. Glue the tomb to the burlap. Glue the stone beside the open door with the lines on the cardboard going in the opposite direction from the tomb.

7. Glue pressed leaves around the tomb.

8. Use markers to decorate the open tomb entrance pattern (He Is Risen). Glue it on the tomb.

9. Tape a paper clip to the back of the picture for hanging.

10. Let your picture remind you of the angel's message "Jesus is alive!"

Other Ideas:

1. Glue squares of colored tissue paper around the open tomb.

2. Draw an angel inside the tomb.

3. Add pressed flowers to the picture.

Patterns

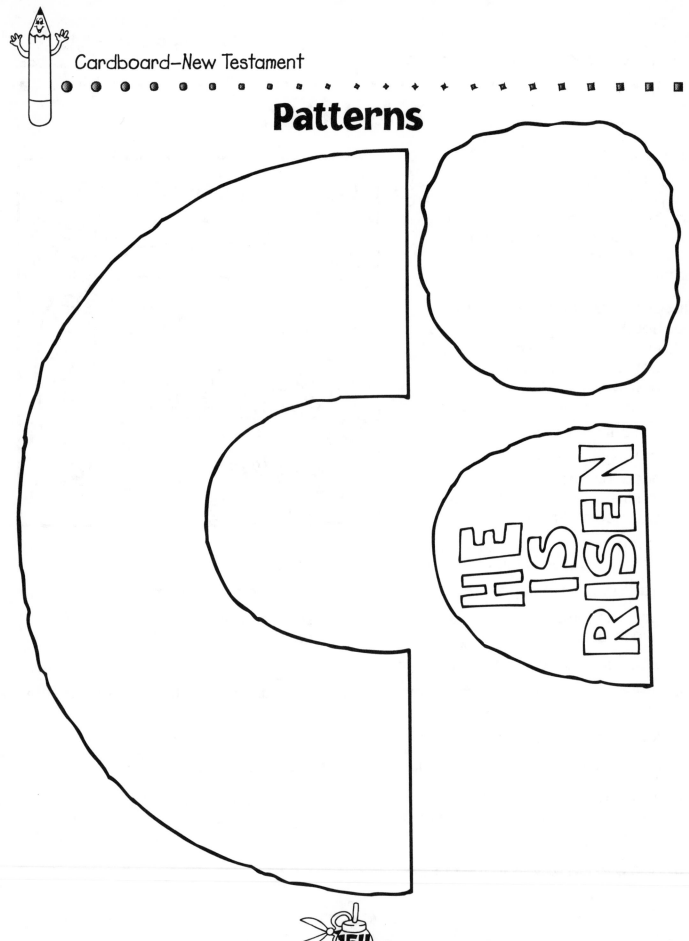

HE IS RISEN

© Shining Star Publications

Suddenly a sound like the blowing of a violent wind came from heaven and filled the whole house where they were sitting. (Acts 2:2)

The Holy Spirit Comes

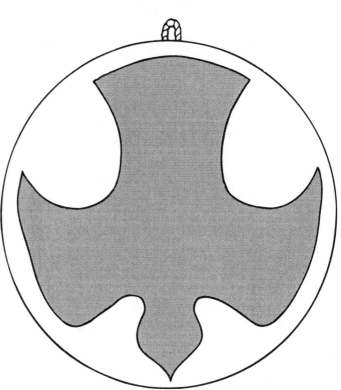

Materials:
cardboard
rice
red food coloring
bowl
glue
tray
yarn
scissors
pencil
pattern on page 156

Directions:

1. Cut out the circle pattern and trace around it on a piece of cardboard. Cut out the cardboard circle.

2. Cut out the dove shape and trace around it on the cardboard circle.

3. Punch a hole at the top of the cardboard circle and tie a loop of yarn through it for a hanger.

4. Dye rice in a bowl with a mixture of red food coloring and water. Spread the rice on a tray to dry.

5. Spread glue on the dove shape and sprinkle white rice on it.

6. Spread glue around the dove shape on the cardboard and sprinkle red rice on it for a background.

7. Talk about how the Holy Spirit, who appeared as a dove at Jesus' baptism, came to Jesus' followers at Pentecost.

Other Idea:
Enlarge the dove shape and put it on a round pizza cardboard.

Pattern

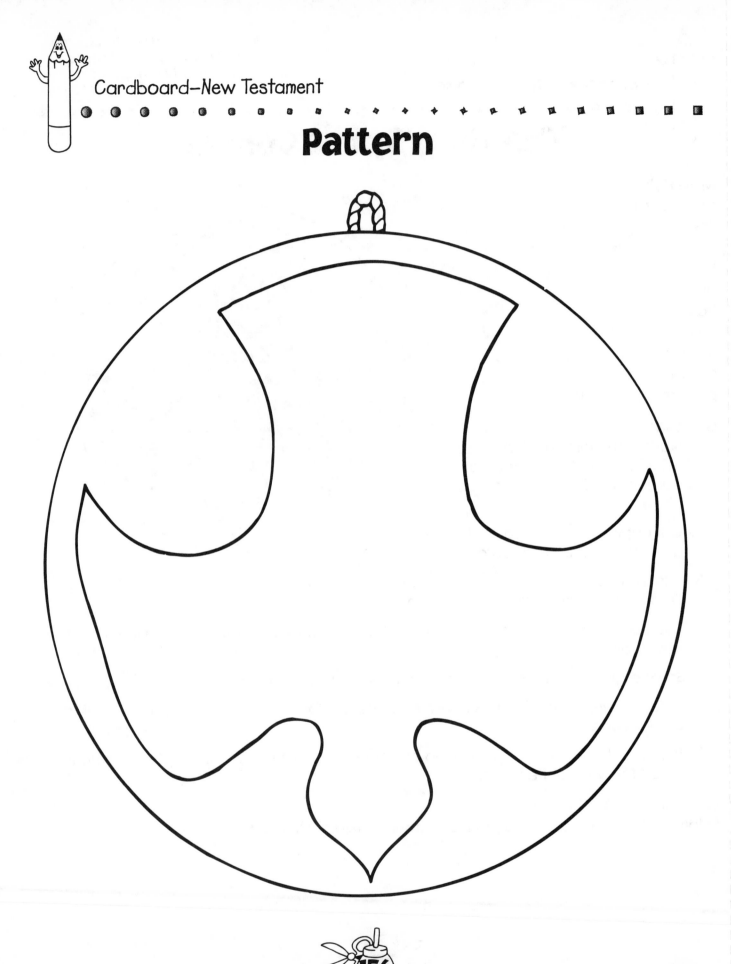

© Shining Star Publications

SS20001

. . . the Holy Spirit said, "Set apart for me Barnabas and Saul for the work to which I have called them."
(Acts 13:2)

Spread the Good Word

Materials:
corrugated cardboard
tempera paint and paintbrush (optional)
two 8" drinking straws
scissors
glue
pencil
stapler
oil-based clay
markers or crayons
patterns on pages 158–159

Directions:
1. Cut out the patterns.

2. Trace around the boat hull and sail shapes on corrugated cardboard and cut them out.

3. Fold up the two sides of the boat and staple the ends together.

4. Paint the boat and sail with tempera paint (optional). Let dry.

5. Use markers to decorate the "Spread the Good Word" pattern pieces. Glue the words on the sail.

6. Staple the two straws together to make a capital "T."

7. Fold the top of the sail over the top straw and staple in place. Glue the sail along the vertical straw.

8. Stick the end of the straw in a ball of oil-based clay and set it in the middle of the boat.

9. Look through Acts 13–28 to find some of the places Paul went to spread God's Word. Talk about ways missionaries travel today to spread God's Word.

Other Ideas:
1. Use colored posterboard for the boat and sail. Add lettering and boat details with markers.

2. Accordion-fold a piece of construction paper for a sail or use it straight.

© Shining Star Publications

SS20001

Pattern

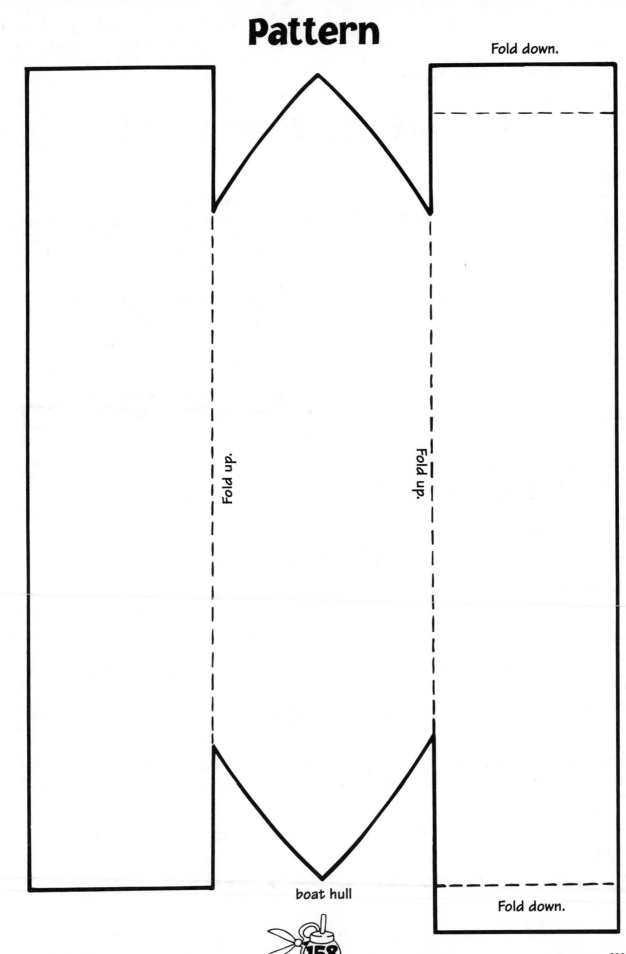

Fold down.

Fold up.

Fold up.

boat hull

Fold down.

© Shining Star Publications

158

SS20001

Patterns

boat sail

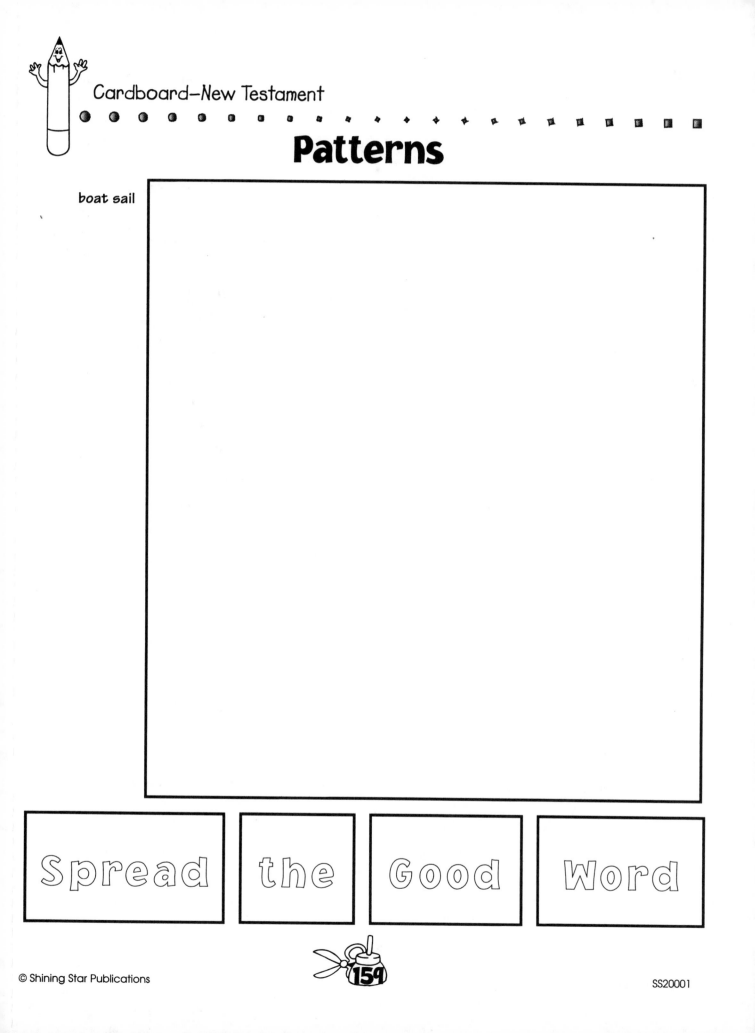

Spread | the | Good | Word

© Shining Star Publications

SS20001

. . . *"Believe in the Lord Jesus,*
and you will be saved . . ."
(Acts 16:31)

Believe in Jesus

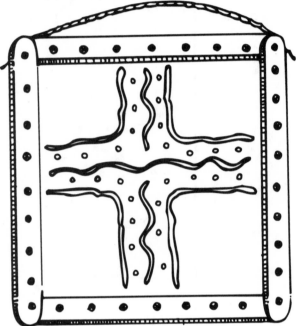

Materials:

posterboard, colored glue, scissors, eight craft sticks (4½" long), yarn, glue, ruler

Directions:

1. Cut a 4½" x 4½" square of posterboard.

2. Glue four craft sticks around the square as indicated in the diagram. Glue the last four sticks on the back.

3. Use colored glue to draw a cross in the square. Draw lines or dots in the cross shape. Use colored glue to decorate the craft sticks, if you wish.

4. Cut an 8" piece of yarn. Tie it to each side of the top for a hanger.

5. Let your cross picture serve as a reminder of Paul and Silas' words in Acts 16:31 to the jailer at Philippi, . . . *"Believe in the Lord Jesus, and you will be saved . . ."*

Other Ideas:

1. Use markers to draw a picture inside the frame.

2. Make a cross out of pieces of yarn.

3. Glue a picture from an old Christmas card inside the frame.

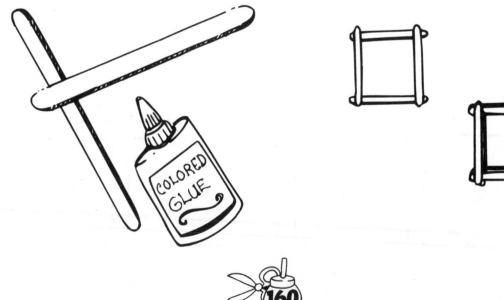

© Shining Star Publications